Tournamen
for Advanced

By

David Sklansky

A product of Two Plus Two Publishing
www.twoplustwo.com

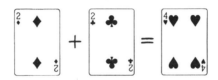

SECOND EDITION

FIRST PRINTING
MAY 2003

Printing and Binding
Creel Printing Co.
Las Vegas, Nevada

Printed in the United States of America

Tournament Poker for Advanced Players

For information contact: **Two Plus Two Publishing
226 Garfield Dr.
Henderson NV 89074
(702) 896-1326**

ISBN: 1-880685-28-0

To Dr. Jack Henri Vitenson

The Best Urologist in America

Thanks for giving me all
the extra years with my dad.

Table of Contents

About David Sklansky

David Sklansky is generally considered the number one authority on gambling in the world today. Besides his ten books on the subject, David also has produced two videos and numerous writings for various gaming publications. His occasional poker seminars always receive an enthusiastic reception, including those given at the Taj Mahal in Atlantic City and the World Series of Poker in Las Vegas.

More recently, David has been doing consulting work for casinos, Internet gaming sites, and gaming device companies. He has recently invented several games, soon to appear in casinos.

David attributes his standing in the gambling community to three things:

1. The fact that he presents his ideas as simply as possible (sometimes with Mason Malmuth) even though these ideas frequently involve concepts that are deep, subtle, and not to be found elsewhere.

2. The fact that the things he says and writes can be counted on to be accurate.

3. The fact that to this day a large portion of his income is still derived from gambling (usually poker, but occasionally blackjack, sports betting, horses, video games, casino promotions, or casino tournaments).

Thus, those who depend on David's advice know that he still depends on it himself.

Other Books by David Sklansky

Hold 'em Poker
The Theory of Poker
Getting The Best of It
Sklansky on Poker
Poker, Gaming, and Life
Sklansky Talks Blackjack

Gambling for a Living by David Sklansky and Mason Malmuth
Hold 'em Poker for Advanced Players by David Sklansky and Mason Malmuth
Seven-Card Stud for Advanced Players by David Sklansky, Mason Malmuth, and Ray Zee

Introduction

When I started playing poker for a living, poker tournaments did not exist. Then about 30 years ago, the Horseshoe Casino in Las Vegas came up with an idea which they called the World Series of Poker. The World Series of Poker offered a poker tournament every other day as well as incredible high stakes side action. For many years the only poker tournament (actually a collection of tournaments) was, in fact, the World Series of Poker. The final event was a $10,000 no-limit hold 'em tournament. The winner of that tournament was crowned the World Champion of Poker. Thirty some years later, the winner of that tournament is still regarded by most people as the world champion.

A few years after the World Series of Poker started, a small number of other casinos decided to offer their own collection of tournaments. These included Amarillo Slim's Super Bowl of Poker, originally held at Lake Tahoe, and the Stairway to the Stars poker tournament held at the Stardust in Las Vegas. Like the World Series of Poker, they had a final event that cost $5,000 or $10,000 to enter, and a series of smaller events that usually cost between $300 and $2,000 to enter. This was the tournament situation for quite a few years; three or four major events, including the World Series of Poker, that broke up the monotony of the day-to-day games that serious poker players had to endure.

Then about ten years ago, poker tournaments exploded in their availability. Those who preferred tournaments over sidegames could find a decent sized tournament to play almost any day of the year. Some, in fact, chose to do just that, traveling around the country, playing in event after event. (Other professional poker players also followed the "tournament trail," not to play in the events themselves, but to play in the "sidegames" that spring up around the tournaments.) In fact, tournaments have now become so popular that small buy-in events

1

(usually between \$20-to-\$100) are a common feature of many cardrooms.

The question, of course, is whether there is good money to be made playing tournaments. The short answer is yes. There is no doubt that the better players have a definite long run edge (or what gamblers call a positive EV). Furthermore, this edge is significant, and can add up to a lot of money, as long as the buy-in is substantial. There are, however, three major downsides to concentrating on tournament play for your livelihood. They are:

1. There is great volatility to your short term results. If, for example, you are good enough to win a 100 player tournament once every 40 tries, on average, you can go an awful long time before you get that win.

2. To be a serious tournament player requires a willingness to travel all over the country, or even the world.

3. When you play in a tournament, you cannot play in a regular ring game. There are many players who can beat tournaments who would still be better off in the long run playing in a normal game.

In spite of the three aforementioned downsides, the fact is that serious poker players should, at least occasionally, consider playing in a poker tournament. Not only because of the positive EV involved, but also because of the chance of a score, and the fact that a change of routine can never hurt once in awhile. But if you are going to play in a tournament, it stands to reason you should play that tournament as well as possible. Most good players don't. That is what this book is for.

So what exactly will this book show you? It will explain how your play should differ when in a tournament from how you play in a regular game. Every other book that has attempted to do that, up until this point, is either flawed or incomplete. This book will show you exactly where strategy changes, compared to normal games, are indicated, and why.

What this book will not do, however, is teach you how to play good poker. It assumes that you already do that. The changes that you make in a tournament won't help you much if you don't already play well. If you are not yet at that level where you can beat medium sized poker games, you need to study *The Theory of Poker, Hold 'em Poker for Advanced Players, Seven-Card Stud for Advanced Players, High-Low-Split Poker for Advanced Players,* and other appropriate books published by Two Plus Two Publishing LLC.

If you already play well, you would probably show a small long run profit making absolutely no adjustments for the fact that you are in a tournament. The reason being that most of the other players don't play as well as you. However, your failure to make adjustments will cost you a lot of money.

Using This Book

This book is a little different from other books in the *for Advanced Players* series in that it assumes you already know how to play poker well. If that's not the case, you will need to read and study those titles mentioned in the "Introduction."

But if you already have a good understanding of how to play poker well and want to expand into tournament poker, this is certainly the book to study. However, although I say study, it is recommended that the whole book be read first, after which you can return to those sections that require more effort.

Once you feel that your understanding of this material is fairly complete, you should then concentrate on the "Hand Quizzes." Having a good understanding of proper tournament strategy and being able to implement it "in the heat of battle," are not always the same thing. The quizzes will help in this area and many of you will find it to be the most important part of the book.

As with all forms of poker, I don't recommend that you immediately buy in to a large limit event. Even though the strategies in this book are designed with these events in mind, it is still better to start lower and work your way up. However, if you enter and win a low cost satellite, that puts you in one of these events, I certainly have no problem with that.

Keep in mind, as the text emphasizes, that proper poker tournament strategy and proper sidegame strategy are sometimes very different. For example, it might be that a hand which should be played for a raise in a sidegame, should be mucked in a tournament. One of the keys to successful tournament play is to recognize these situations and make the appropriate adjustments, even if it doesn't (at first) feel quite right.

Note: Cards designated in the text are either underlined or not. If a card is underlined, then it is a hole card in a stud hand; otherwise it is either an upcard or not part of a stud hand. For

6 Using This Book

example, if you see A♣A♠ and we are talking about hold 'em, this is representing a starting hand of two black aces. If you see A♣A♠A♥, then this is a starting stud hand of three aces and the two black aces are down.

Why Play
Tournament Poker?

To reiterate, this book is written for someone who has a good understanding of standard ring game poker. Assuming that's the case, you will already be winning at the poker table. So why venture into the tournament arena?

The answer is easy. As I stated in the "Introduction," there is good money to be made in tournaments; there is a chance for a big score; and a change in routine can keep you fresh.

You win at tournament poker because of two important factors. First, some of your opponents play poker badly, and in extreme cases literally give their money away. This includes players who consistently lose in sidegames, and now, perhaps out of frustration, want to give tournaments a shot. In most cases, their results will be the same.

The second reason you can win money playing tournament poker is this form of poker will offer numerous opportunities for the expert player to make adjustments from standard sidegame strategy. Many of your opponents, even those who play poker fairly well, do not understand what these adjustments are, or fail to implement them correctly. This will sometimes cause them to make serious errors, especially late in an event, which you can take advantage of.

I mentioned earlier that the risk factor in tournaments is very high. That is "there is great volatility to your short term results."[1] You may also need to travel, and when in a tournament, you can't play a ring game. So tournaments, especially on a day-in and day-out basis, are not for everyone.

---

[1] See my book *Poker, Gaming, & Life* for more discussion.

8 Why Play Tournament Poker?

Nonetheless, besides their long term profitability they can be very exciting to play. This is especially true when you have reached the final table and so much is riding on the turn of a card.

So given the tremendous growth of poker tournaments, and the fact that they are here to stay, there's no reason not to join in. They may or may not be right for you everyday, but they can certainly be worth your time on occasion.

Part One

Getting Started

Getting Started
Introduction

Before you play a poker tournament you need to know how a tournament works and how it differs from a sidegame. We'll see that if you have chips, you can't quit (unless you manage to get them all) and if you run out of chips, you must quit (assuming you are not in what is known as the rebuy period that some tournaments offer). In addition, we'll see that winning all the chips does not get you all the money, and that you might still win a substantial prize even though you have lost every chip that you started with.

But most important, I'll start to talk about how these factors not only impact your strategy, but how they frequently affect the way your opponents play, which should also impact your strategy. As already mentioned, not only are tournaments different from standard poker, but proper tournament strategy, can be quite a bit different as well.

How a Poker
Tournament Works

I assume that most people who are reading this book are very familiar with the rules of poker tournaments, so this will be short and sweet. If you are not, there are many other sources where more detailed information is available.

In a typical tournament, everyone enters for the same amount of money, say $500. The house usually charges an extra "entry fee,"say $30, which they pocket. The total prize pool, comprised of the $500 buy-ins are distributed to the winner, second place, third place, down to whatever the rules of the tournament specify. (Often 18, 20, or more places on occasion.) If, for example, this tournament had 200 entries, there would be a $100,000 total prize pool. At the beginning of the tournament, each player would receive $500 in chips. (Sometimes the non-negotiable chips have a face value different from the actual buy-in, but that is of no consequence, and is readjusted at the end of the tournament.)

Usually a tournament involves just one game. It may be limit hold 'em, no-limit hold 'em, seven-card stud, or Omaha high-low-split eight-or-better. Occasionally, the tournament involves multiple games that are changed after a specified time period. The stakes start out fairly small in comparison to the buy-in. In the $500 example, they may start out at the $10-$20 or $15-$30 level. With 200 entries there might be twenty ten handed tables, all playing those stakes. As time goes by, the stakes are raised. Typically, they are raised once an hour. In the example given, the second hour might be $20-$40, followed by $30-$60, $50-$100, $75-$150, $100-$200, etc. Players who go broke are eliminated. (There are some tournaments that allow a player who goes broke to buy in again during a specified time period early in the tournament. The principles discussed in this book will assume generally that the tournament is either not a rebuy tournament or that you have passed the point where rebuys are allowed. There will, however, be a short chapter discussing how this aspect of tournaments should be handled.)

As players go broke, tables are broken up and combined. (Most well run tournaments break up tables in a pre-specified order. Knowing when your table will be broken up can be helpful to your tournament strategy, as we will discuss later).

The tournament does not end until one person has all the chips. In the old days, that person won everything. He would have walked away with $100,000 in our example. Later on casinos realized that they were much better off spreading the money around. They experimented briefly with stopping the tournament when a certain number of players were left, and letting those players keep what they had in front of them. For instance, they might stop this particular tournament when five players were left, and the winner would be the one who had the most chips, maybe $40,000, fifth place would have the least chips, maybe $1,500, and everybody would keep what they had. Tournaments like that are extremely rare nowadays. They require a somewhat different strategy and will not be discussed in this book

The way tournaments are paid off now works like this: Once again, the tournament does not end until one player has all the chips. However, that player no longer wins all the money. Instead, the casino makes note of what point each player becomes eliminated, and pays off based on that. The last player to be eliminated wins second prize, the next to last player wins third prize, and so on. In most tournaments, prizes are awarded to everyone who makes the last table. Those tournaments with many entries often award prizes to those who make it to the next to last table. The World Series of Poker final event pays something to those who reach the last five tables! The prizes are a pre-specified percentage of the total prize money. For example, if this $500 tournament was a hold 'em tournament that paid ten places, first prize might be 30 percent of the total prize pool, second prize might be 20 percent, followed by 13, 10, 7, 6, 5, 4, 3, and 2 percent respectively. If two people were eliminated simultaneously they would share their prizes, or in some tournaments, the larger prize would go to the player who started that hand with more chips.

How Poker Tournaments are Different

There are many reasons why you cannot simply play your normal, tough poker strategy, and expect to extract the maximum amount from a poker tournament. The fact is that poker tournaments are different from regular games. How they are different and what that means for your optimum strategy will be discussed in detail in subsequent chapters. For now, I just want to list these differences.

1. You must quit if you lose what you have in front of you.

2. They must quit if they lose what they have in front of them.

3. The stakes are constantly raised. (Thus, "advertising" plays can reap bigger rewards than usual).

4. You will often be faced with situations in which you or your opponent is "all-in" before all of the cards are out.

5. Your table will be broken up, and in many tournaments you will know about when that will happen.

6. When you have a very short stack, you must consider whether you can afford to wait for a normally good starting hand.

7. Hourly rate considerations do not apply.

8. Other players' stack sizes have great significance, especially at the end of a tournament.

9. Hands played between other opponents are very significant, even when you are not in that hand.

10. Because of the way prizes are distributed, your goals differ from what they would in a regular game. For example, in theory, you could finish second place without ever having more chips than you started with.

EV

Many times in this book I will use the term EV. It is an abbreviation for the words *expected value*. Every bet has an expected value, either positive, negative, or zero. Basically, expected value means the amount you will win or lose per bet if you could somehow make it a large number of times.

For instance, if someone stupidly offered you $300-to-$200 on a flip of a coin, you have an expected value of positive $50. Why? Because after many such bets you would be ahead an average of $50 per bet. Had you made 10 bets, you would average winning five and losing five, putting you up $500, or $50 per bet.

$$\$500 = (5)(\$300) - (5)(\$200)$$

$$\$50 = \left(\frac{\$500}{10}\right)$$

If someone offered you $1,320-to-$200, against your rolling a seven with two dice, you figure to win $1,320 one time, while losing $200 five times. (Since rolling seven is a 1-in-6 shot [or 5-to-1 against.)] That puts you up $320 after six times, which is a positive EV of $53.33.

$$\$320 = (1)(\$1,320) - (5)(\$200)$$

$$53.33 = \frac{\$329}{6}$$

So the dice bet has a higher expected value than the coin flip bet, and would usually be the one you would take if you could only take one.

It is not necessary that the EV of a bet can be calculated so precisely in order for it to be thought of in those terms. For instance, when playing $10-20 hold 'em, we could speculate on what the EV of a pair of aces on the button is. Depending on the game and your skill level, I would suspect that it is around $60.

We could also speculate on the EV of two alternate plays with the same hand. What is the EV of calling with

Jc Tc

under the gun, as compared with the EV of raising with it from the same position? (Folding has an obvious EV of zero.)

In all of these cases we are simply talking about the average amount per hand you will win (or lose) if you were to play the hand that way many times in the same situation. Experienced players will have a good idea as to what these numbers truly are, and they can play an important part in your overall winning strategy.

In this book, EV is mentioned frequently because it turns out that in a tournament it is not always right to choose the play with the slightly higher EV. This is because the higher EV bet may be more likely to lose. In the dice example, your $53.33 EV came with a bet that would lose five-sixths of the time. The $50 EV coin flip bet involved something that would lose only half the time. Assuming that you have enough money to withstand short-term fluctuations, it is always better to choose the bet with the higher EV. But if you do not have that cushion, it may well be right to choose the slightly smaller EV if that bet will win more often, especially if going broke keeps you from making more positive EV bets.

Notice, that may well be your situation in a poker tournament. Balancing your quest for extra EV and your quest for survival is a major factor in proper tournament strategy. In a sidegame, this will not be a major consideration since you should almost always have enough money to keep playing (even if you have to reach into your pocket for more). That will often not be the case in a tournament and we will shortly see that some of those standard sidegame plays that you are used to making, are not always correct at the tournament table.

You're Broke
— You're Done

Aside from the early stages of a rebuy tournament, the fact is that losing all your chips is worse in a tournament than it is in a regular game. There are two reasons for this. One has to do with the way tournaments are paid. Your prize money depends solely on the point at which you were eliminated, not how much you had when you were eliminated. Thus, it is especially catastrophic to go broke when only a few people are left. For instance, suppose four players are left, you have the second largest amount of chips and get busted by the chip leader. You come in fourth, while the other two players move up in standings simply by watching you lose your money.

We will have more to say later about the proper strategy for the times you make the last table, but for now you can see that in situations like this, there is a great incentive to avoid going broke, especially with debatable, mildly profitable hands. To give an extreme example, suppose on the last day of the $10,000 No-Limit Hold 'em World Championship at the World Series of Poker there were four players left, the two shortest stacks had about $30,000 each, you had $200,000 and the leader was sitting on millions of dollars of chips. Suppose you foolishly played against that big chip leader and lost everything. That cost you over a half a million dollars in prize money considering that you could have probably antied your way into second place.

The above factor (which would indicate that you avoid close gambles with a slight advantage, to keep from going broke) only takes on significance near the very end of a tournament. But there is another reason to eschew close gambles even early on. This reason has nothing to do with the prize structure, and in fact is something you should be aware of even if the tournament paid only one winner. What I am speaking of involves the presumption that you are one of the best players in the tournament. That being the case, you should avoid close gambles, especially for large portions of your chips. It may seem that giving up a positive EV gamble can never be right. However, even from a purely mathematical standpoint, you sometimes should.

For instance, suppose I knew that tomorrow someone would offer me \$200-to-\$100 on a coin flip. Meanwhile, today someone offers me \$120-to-\$100 on a coin flip. The problem is that I only have \$100 to my name, and will not be able to play tomorrow if I lose today. If I take the first bet, I will miss out on the opportunity for the second bet, half the time.

If I take the first bet, along with the second bet if I have the money, I will be broke half the time, I will have profited \$20 one-fourth of the time, and profited \$320 the other fourth of the time. That is a positive EV of \$35.

$$\$35 = \left(\frac{1}{2}\right)(-\$100) + \left(\frac{1}{4}\right)(\$20) + \left(\frac{1}{4}\right)(\$320)$$

If instead I wait until tomorrow, I'll be broke half the time and end up \$200 the other half. That is an EV of \$50.

$$\$50 = \left(\frac{1}{2}\right)(-\$100) + \left(\frac{1}{2}\right)(\$200)$$

So you can see that it can be mathematically correct to pass up a good bet if losing that bet can keep you from making an even better bet later on.

There are two different ways this can apply to poker situations.

One, you have a heads-up situation with a hand that is only barely worth playing EV wise. For example, playing no-limit hold 'em, if a player moves all-in with what you somehow know is you would seriously consider throwing away

getting barely above even money, if losing that pot would get you broke or near broke. This, in spite of the fact that two fours is a tiny favorite over ace-king suited.

Other close heads-up situations that you might opt to fold would involve getting pot odds that are just a tad above that which you need to give you a positive EV. In other words, you might not take 4.3-to-1 on a 4-to-1 shot. Since saving a bet gives you more ammunition.

A more important example of this concept involves choosing whether to play a hand multiway as opposed to heads-up or short handed. Put another way, you may have a decision whether to slowplay a good hand. Well, once again assuming you are one of the best players in the tournament, the answer is that most prospective slowplays should not be made. Unless you have a "monster" hand, slowplaying, while often making you more when it works, entails an extra risk of losing the pot. This risk is often worth taking in a regular game, but not in a tournament.

To give a mathematical example, suppose you could choose either to get 100-to-20 odds on a 75 percent shot, or 80-to-40 odds on a 90 percent shot. If you work it out, you will see that the first situation gives you an EV of $70, while the second one gives you an EV of $68.

$$70 = (.75)(100) - (.25)(20)$$

$$68 = (.90)(80) - (.10)(40)$$

However, the second one gives you only a 10 percent chance of losing, while the first one, has a 25 percent chance of losing. Therefore, that second one gives you an extra 15 percent chance of not only losing that $20, but also the $80 that you could have won. It is almost definitely worth giving up $2 in EV to avoid this disaster in a poker tournament. Notice that this example is equivalent to suggesting that you raise $20 and get two calls, compared to calling $20 and getting five calls. Situations like this come up all the time. Slowplaying in these situations is often wrong, even early in the tournament (when you are a top player), and almost definitely wrong late in a tournament.[2]

Please do not misunderstand what I am saying here. My point is that, if you are one of the best players in the tournament, you should usually not risk significant money on very close decisions. But those decisions must be close. (Also, as we will soon see, the decisions I am speaking of involve situations where someone else has already bet.) If it's close, fold hands where calls might be a very slight positive EV, and raise (if that will knock players out) where a slowplaying call might have a very slightly higher EV. But again, remember, that these strategy deviations, especially early in the tournament, assume you are one of the best players in the tournament.

---

[2] Yet in a sidegame where you can always reach into your pocket for more money, this exact same play is usually absolutely correct.

There are also quite a few exceptions to the above. Here are some reasons why you might choose *not* to stay away from close decisions:

1. There is a juicy sidegame that you would love to play in if you get knocked out of the tournament. Obviously, in a case like this, your inclination would be to either quickly increase your stack, or to go broke. If that is so, you would not only be glad to risk significant tournament chips with a slight edge, you might even want to do it with a disadvantage.

2. Hourly rate means something to you. We will go into this further in another chapter. Simply put, tournament players are not usually concerned about their hourly rate. They just want to maximize their average profit per tournament. This is different from their average profit per hour played in the tournament. But if for some reason, your hourly rate in the tournament matters, (usually because there is another tournament or sidegame you'll get into if you go broke) then avoiding close gambles, when you have a little bit the best of it, may no longer be worth doing.

3. You are concerned about your future image. Any time you can deceive your opponents at lower stakes to the point where they will make a mistake against you once the stakes are raised, you gain a lot from that deception. Thus, you may not want to tip off your opponents early on that you are avoiding close gambles, lest they take advantage of that later on when the stakes have increased.

4. You may want to take high pot odds with a bit the worst of it. The idea of avoiding close gambles to reduce your chances of going broke doesn't really apply to situations in which

your risk is small. For instance, seeing the flop with

getting debatable odds. There are certain psychological and technical advantages to significantly increasing your stack early on, and as long as your EV is not really negative and your risk is small, this could be a gamble worth taking.

5. You have the smallest stack at the last table. There will be a full chapter on last table strategy. For now, understand that when you have the smallest stack, most of your opponents will be playing conservatively, hoping you go broke, which will move them up the prize ladder. Because of this, you must take chances, since your only real hope is to get lucky somewhere along the line. (Keep in mind however, that this concept totally reverses if other smaller stacks are foolishly playing too loosely. In that case the principles of this chapter would hold even more than usual. In other words, in a situation like that, you would stay away from any gamble even remotely close, so that it would be you who moves up the prize ladder.)

6. Again, the avoidance of gambles mentioned in this chapter relates to when someone else has bet. When you are the original bettor or raiser, you will not play *fewer* hands than you would in a normal game, but in fact, most likely play *more*. The reason, as we will see next chapter, is that your opponents are just as worried as you are about going broke.

They're Broke
— They're Done

(First, let me remind you that we are assuming either a no rebuy tournament or a tournament where the option to rebuy has expired. Proper strategy when the rebuy option is on may be rather different from what we will discuss below.)

The fact is that almost everyone who plays a tournament is playing more cautiously than usual because, unlike a sidegame, they cannot continue to play if they lose all their chips. The only exceptions are those who have already garnered quite a few chips, or players who are not taking the tournament that seriously. Thus, it is quite common to see a player who is notorious for his looseness in normal games playing significantly tighter when he has a small or moderate stack in a poker tournament. Ironically, these players are probably making a mistake. Only the very best players should be avoiding slightly positive gambles to allow their bigger edges time to accumulate. The typical tournament player should not ever turn down any situation with the smallest of edges. You could even argue that he should gamble in situations where he has slightly the worst of it. But that is not the way the vast majority of mediocre tournament players operate. Perhaps it is because they want to experience as much time in the tournament as possible. But whatever the reason, the fact is that your opponents will, in general, play quite a bit tighter in the tournament than they play in sidegames.

In my introduction I said that if you are an excellent player, and you simply play your normal game, you will show a long run profit playing tournaments.[3] Strictly speaking, that statement is

---

[3] A smaller profit, of course, than if you implement the ideas in this book.

true, but only because it is assumed that your normal excellent game includes adjusting for your opponents' surprising tightness. In other words, I am assuming that as a great player you notice how tightly they are playing, and you play accordingly. If instead you played your normal game without adjusting to that tightness in your opponents, you would not beat tournaments.

The fact is that the single biggest change between proper sidegame strategy and proper tournament strategy arises from the fact that your opponents typically play much differently when in tournaments than in sidegames. The most successful tournament players use this fact to their utmost advantage. In a nutshell, what they do is aggressively go after small pots and quickly back off at the first sign of strength from their opponents.

Many tournament experts cannot beat tough sidegames because they don't know how to play multiway pots, and don't know how to play against players who are willing to gamble it up. But these situations are rare in tournaments. A large part of their edge simply comes from understanding something I call the "Gap Concept."

The Gap Concept

The last two chapters would seem to pull you in two different directions as far as your general strategy in a tournament. "You're Broke — You're Done" would tend to indicate that you should play tighter than normal. "They're Broke — They're Done" would tend to indicate you should play looser than normal. Is there a way to reconcile these two apparently contradictory forces?

There is a very important general principle understood by all good poker players. That is, you need a better hand to play against someone who has already opened the betting than you would need to open yourself. For instance, in jacks-or-better draw poker you might open with a pair of queens, but you would never call someone who has already opened when you hold those same two queens. In limit hold 'em, you would most certainly raise in middle position with

especially if no one else was in yet but you would rarely play against an early position raiser with that same hand.

The difference between the hand you need to call an opener with, and that with which you would open yourself, I call the "Gap." How wide that Gap is depends on how tight your opponents play. If your opponents are quite loose, there may be no gap at all. Playing lowball draw in middle position, you can open with:

a one card draw to a smooth eight. But you would normally call an opener only with a one-card draw to a smooth seven. If however, the opener is extremely loose, you can call him with that eight draw. Likewise, you could play against a very loose early position hold 'em raiser with the same minimum hands that you yourself would open raise with.

So, it should be obvious that the Gap can range from non-existent to quite high. And, in a tournament, this Gap is often extremely high. In other words, in a tournament it is often right to open raise with hands far inferior to those with which you would need to call someone else who open raised.

If you think about it, you should see that this strategy coincides perfectly with the principles of the first two chapters. You avoid confrontations with those who have already shown strength, and you take advantage of those who are trying to preserve their chips. Here are a couple of examples:

1. In limit hold 'em, if three people fold, you should probably raise with:

or

On the other hand, in this same position, if the under the gun player has raised, you should often consider folding a hand as good as

or

2. In stud, if no one except the bring-in has entered the pot, you should usually raise with the highest upcard showing (not duplicated elsewhere), but if someone else raises, you should usually fold any pair lower than the denomination of the upcard that had raised, especially if your kicker is also lower. In addition, you should be less apt to play drawing hands,

such as

or three straights, since your pot and implied odds would usually be less than they would be in a sidegame

Believe it or not, this one strategy adjustment, along with otherwise good play, accounts for about half of the extra success top tournament players have, compared to good sidegame players who don't increase their "Gap."

Of course, there are exceptions to the Gap Concept. For one, you must be aware of what kind of players are behind you and what kind of situations they are in. If the players behind you have either a very small or very large stack, loosening up on your normal opening requirements may be unwise. Players with small stacks are often ready to give up, and will therefore be quite apt to call you. Players with large stacks are no longer worried about going broke, so they too are probably playing less tightly than they were earlier.

The exception to the other side of the Gap Concept (where someone else has opened) will occur if the raiser in front of you has a lot of chips, or if he is not worried about going broke, *or* if he himself is aware of the Gap Concept. Against players like that, you are giving up too much if you significantly tighten up compared to your normal playing strategy.

As important as the Gap Concept is anytime in a tournament, it becomes more important still with the Gap usually widening even more during the last stages of the tourney. The reason is related to the way prizes are paid. This will be explored in more detail in the chapter called "Prize Structure Implications" at the beginning of the next section.

Getting Started
Afterthought

Mathematical expectation covers any gamble. Generally speaking, if you have the best of it, you want to bet (or raise). But there is an important exception. This occurs when your bankroll is not large enough to withstand the natural fluctuations of the game at hand. When that happens, you should pass on some bets.

This is exactly what happens in tournament poker. Your bankroll, since it is limited to what you can buy-in for, becomes top priority. Thus, you need to understand the implications of "You're Broke — You're Done" and "They're Broke — They're Done," and how all of this affects "The Gap Concept." Ignoring this area will keep your long term results only marginally profitable at best, even if you are an otherwise excellent player.

Of course, there is more to tournament strategy than just understanding how the potential to go broke can, and should, affect play. These other important factors will be covered in the rest of this text. But the previous three chapters are extremely important, and if they were not totally clear, I suggest that you read them again, and again, until they are.

Part Two

Tournament Theory

Tournament Theory
Introduction

Even though this section of the book is called "Tournament Theory" we are already well into that subject. But there is more to tournaments than just the Gap Concept and the avoidance of going broke. Those ideas are extremely important, but they are not the only forces that impact what your proper strategy should be and how your play should sometimes stray from proper sidegame strategy.

So what are some of the additional aspects of a poker tournament that cause you to make strategy adjustments? They include the prize structure, how the chips change value, the impact of your table being broken up, rising stakes, different stack sizes, being all-in, getting close to the money, and final table play.

None of these factors have much impact, if any, on how you should play in a standard sidegame. But poker tournaments are a different story. We'll see that sometimes you should play hyper aggressively and what may look to the unknowledgeable opponent as almost "maniacal," while at other times you should play what is usually called (derogatorily) "weak tight." In fact both these tactics are part of an overall "tough" tournament strategy.

Prize Structure Implications

In the old days, tournaments often ended with a specified number of players keeping what they had in front of them. In tournaments like these, there was little advantage to surviving with a few chips, since it was only the value of those few chips that you kept. In any case, casinos preferred offering tournaments that went down to one player, since they were more dramatic. But since they wanted to give out more than first prize, they devised a scheme where each prize was a certain percentage of the total buy-in. And the prize you won depended solely on how many players were still playing when you were eliminated. It did not matter how much money you had remaining before that last hand.

One result of this prize structure scheme is that you have a major interest in the outcome of hands that you are not in. With few exceptions, it is to your advantage for someone else to go broke. Thus, when a large stack is playing against a small stack, you are usually rooting for the large stack.

The above is pretty much common sense. But I want to take you through a simple mathematical example to demonstrate just how clear cut this is.

Suppose there are three people left in the tournament. They each have $1,000 in front of them. First prize is 60 percent of the total ($1,800). Second prize is 30 percent ($900). Third prize is 10 percent ($300). All three players play equally well. Therefore, on average, each player would (if this situation was repeated a large number of times) obviously go home with $1,000.

$$\$1,000 = \frac{\$3,000}{3}$$

Now, suppose you are one of these three players, and the other two move all-in against each other. When the hand is over, you will have second place locked up, and you will be facing someone who has $2,000. In such a situation, your chances of winning is one out of three, since you have a third of the chips.[4] That means that you will go home with $1,800 one-third of the time, and $900 two-thirds of the time. That's an average of $1,200.

$$\$1,200 = \left(\frac{1}{3}\right)(\$1,800) + \left(\frac{2}{3}\right)(\$900)$$

Before the hand started, your expected pay-off was $1,000. Merely *watching* the other two play against each other, increased your EV by 20 percent, from $1,000 to $1,200. The other two both went down to an average of $900 each

$$\$900 = \frac{\$3,000 - \$1,200}{2}$$

This calculation is very telling. It shows how wonderful it is to sit back and let others go broke, and how bad it is to risk large sums on breakeven situations late in a tournament. In fact, even if you have a decent edge, it could be wrong to gamble. For instance, in the example given, suppose one of the players has a 54 percent chance of winning the heads-up confrontation. If that were so, he will come in third, and win $300 46 percent of the time; he will come in first and win $1,800 36 percent of the time (two-thirds of 54), and he will come in second and win $900 18 percent of the time. Well, that is an average of $948,

---

[4] (See the chapter entitled "Freezeout Calculations.")

$$\$948 = (.46)(\$300) + (.36)(\$1,800) + (.18)(\$900)$$

which means that he still lost \$52 by moving in as a 54 percent favorite. Clearly, this aspect of the tournament must be taken into account, especially when you are fighting for places along the lines of second, third, fourth, and fifth. (Unless, of course, your main goal is to win. If that matters more than the money, throwing away a 54 percent chance of doubling up is almost certainly wrong.)

So what does this all mean?

If you lose money by going all-in, as a 54-to-46 favorite, (and in fact you would have to be above 58.33 percent not to lose money in the specific scenario given) what is one supposed to do? If everybody simply sits back and waits for their opponents to play major pots against each other, nothing will ever happen.

The fact is, though, that you can take advantage of the paradox shown in this chapter. While it is certainly true that calling all-in hurts you if you are 54 percent, and even more so if you are 46 percent, what about if you are the one who makes the first bet? By being the "aggressor" in this situation, you find yourself more likely than usual to win small pots that you bet into (as long as your opponent is familiar with the concepts in this chapter).

For instance, suppose you bet \$2,000 into a \$100 pot, with three of you remaining. If that is about equal to the stack of one of your opponents, he will probably fold a hand he would normally call with, so as not to increase the EV of the third player who is out of the pot. If he did call, he would hurt you even more than he would hurt himself. But unless he is the type to cut off his nose to spite his face, he won't do it. Rather, he will simply wait for those times when he can be the first one to bet, thus putting intolerable pressure on you, since you also do not want to add EV to the player sitting out.

Notice that the Gap Concept, previously discussed, becomes even stronger when the players are in the money or close to it. The

Gap between opening and calling has increased further still. Against players who are aware of the disadvantage of fighting close decisions when others gain by watching, you can aggressively steal small pots, even if they suspect this is what you are doing. But remember that this play assumes not only that your opponent is aware of the concept, but also that he has a moderate amount of chips left. You are more apt to be called if his stack is small or large.

If it is the other player who raises, the calculations of this chapter showed that you need an even better hand than usual to play, even better than you would have at the beginning of the tournament. This is not as true if you know your opponent is aware of the Gap Concept, or if his small or large stack makes it likely he is gambling. But even in these cases, the nature of the prize distribution forces you to often let him succeed in his aggression when he is first. As I said, the Gap discussed earlier typically becomes very wide at the end of a tournament.

I will have more to say about strategy at the end of a tournament later.

When They Call You

This book will not have a real lot to say about later round play. That might surprise those of you who know that I believe most of a good player's profit come in those later rounds. But again, this book is not purporting to teach you how to play winning poker. It is teaching you how to change your winning strategies when you are in a tournament.

And the fact is, most of your strategy changes come early in the hand. That's because the risk of going broke, the prize structure, and the all-in possibilities that influence how you should play in a tournament, have the greatest impact on your early round decisions.

But there is one very important exception. The Gap Concept of the previous chapter has you raising with *more* starting hands than you might normally be used to. It also assumes that they are calling your raises with *fewer* hands. Those two facts have a significant impact on your later round play, especially the very next round.

To properly explain this impact, we must separate seven-card stud from hold 'em or Omaha. More on that in a moment. For now realize that when you take advantage of the Gap Concept, you will sometimes find yourself in a position which you have raised and have been called by a hand that you know is quite a bit better than yours. Even when you have raised with a good hand, you can be fairly sure that those who have called, have a better hand than you are used to facing in this situation. (This chapter is not addressing those times when you get reraised. When that happens your proper strategy is pretty much the same as it would be in a non-tournament.)

We can break things down into three possible situations:

1. They called you when you had a great hand.
2. They called you when you had a good hand.
3. They called you when your hand is below your usual requirements.

In all of these cases their hand can be expected to be better than normal. So how does that impact the next round?

If your hand happens to be quite good, you should be prepared to sandbag more than usual — be more likely to check raise on the next round, or possibly the round after that (either because you check called on the previous round or bet and were called).

Here's an example from seven-card stud. You raise with

and are called by

Since he is more likely than usual to have queens, you should often try for a check raise on fourth or fifth street when you catch non-threatening looking cards.

Here's an example from hold 'em. You raise with

The flop is

You bet (the flop) and get called. You should usually go for a check raise on fourth street.

If your hand is merely good, you should often immediately go into a check calling mode, even though you would tend to be aggressive in a normal sidegame. You are up against a good hand, so if you check, he will probably bet your hand for you, even when it is slightly worse than yours. In some situations it might be right to throw in a raise to find out where you're at, thereby allowing you to get rid of your hand if reraised. But usually simply checking and calling is the preferred strategy.

Hold 'em example: You raise with

get called. The flop is:

Proper tournament strategy is to frequently go into a defensive shell and just check and call. In a standard ring game you would be much more inclined to bet.

If your hand is worse than usual, be prepared to be done with it on the next round. Don't forget, his hand is better than usual. So unless the flop or fourth street has been kind to you, you should usually simply check and fold to a bet on the next round. This goes against normal poker strategy in which the early aggressor almost always fires at least one more "barrel" if he is called. That is usually not right in a tournament where you must take into consideration the necessity of conserving chips, the fact that you are up against a better than usual hand, and the fact that your hand is not as good as it normally would be.

There is, however, an important exception regarding hold 'em and Omaha high-low-split eight-or-better. The exception occurs when ragged small cards come in hold 'em, or big cards in Omaha high-low-split eight-or-better. If your raise is called before the flop in a hold 'em tournament, there is a good chance ragged low cards will not have hit your opponent. Thus if you happen to have one of those semi-steal hands like it is probably worth taking a shot at the pot on the flop when it comes something like

For similar reasons, you should often try to steal the pot from your opponent who called you in Omaha high-low-split eight-or-better when the flop comes two or more high cards.

In stud an exception (to giving up when caught with a weak hand) occurs when you catch scary cards on board, and your opponent doesn't. If you raise with

and get called by a queen, you should certainly bet again if your next card is the K♦. And if you are called, you should probably bet a third time if fifth street is a ten or higher (or a nine or a seven). Otherwise, you should probably check and fold if he bets.

Chips Change Value

Some of you may have heard the idea that each individual chip that you win is worth less than the previous ones. This is a true statement, especially regarding the vast majority of tournaments that pay a fixed prize structure, depending on when you were eliminated.[5]

As an example, if you were playing the $10,000 No-Limit Hold 'em World Championship at the World Series of Poker, and were allowed to sell your chips to an outsider who would take over your seat, how much would those chips be worth to him, assuming he was a typical player who could be expected to break even in the long run. Obviously if he bought them right at the beginning, the answer would be $10,000.

But what the principle in the first sentence is illustrating, is that as your chips increase that bystander should no longer pay you their value to have a fair transaction. The easiest way to show this is to imagine that you have brought your chips all the way up to $3,000,000 (out of the approximately $5,000,000 in total buy-ins). That bystander would be quite dense to pay you even $2,000,000 for those chips, since first prize, as of this writing, is $2,000,000.

(There are however some exceptions to this principle. To give another extreme example, suppose you have brought your $10,000 up to $230,000, and there are only three players left. Since third prize is in the neighborhood of $700,000, you would be the idiot if *you* sold them for face value.)

There is another point. The above example assumes that you are a typical player. Suppose that you are one of the best players in the tournament. Or alternatively, suppose the bystander is. It

---

[5] This was first shown by Mason Malmuth in his book *Gambling Theory and Other Topics*.

might be worth it for him to buy your original $10,000 in chips for $30,000 because of his great skill. And if you increased your $10,000 to $21,000, it might be worth it for him to pay $50,000 for that larger stack.

In other words, the extra $11,000 you won, would allow you to charge him $20,000 more. On the other hand, in this second example, even though your $11,000 win made you $20,000, it did not violate the principle that extra chips won had less value, because your first $10,000 was worth $30,000 (to the bystander anyway), while the second $11,000 was worth less than that.

The bottom line is that, with a few exceptions, what you gain by winning a chip is not quite as much as what you lose, when you lose a chip. We have already covered this idea with different words, and have described the strategy changes that should be employed to take advantage of this concept. I merely wanted to address that often repeated principle and show you where it comes from.

Keeping the Pot Small

There are two more reasons I recommend you do not push small edges early in the hand, unless you have a chance to steal the pot. It is not just that you reduce your risk by saving a bet, it is also that an extra raise on your part changes the nature of the whole hand from that point forward.

An extra raise by you makes the pot bigger, which in turn forces everyone to stay in longer. You might have to take cards off that you would not have had if the pot had been smaller. This increases your volatility. Worse yet, the bigger pots mean that your opponent will chase more often when you have the best hand. And that of course might result in his winning a pot that you would have won. If you are one of the best players in the game, and are trying to maximize your tournament result, this extra volatility is something to avoid.

Another reason to keep the pot small, true both in tournaments and non-tournaments, is that opponents' hands are easier to read. Since they are getting lower odds, the fact that they are staying in ought to allow you to narrow down their possible holdings more than you could if the pot was big. Of course, the same could be said for their being able to read your hand more easily. But as one of the best players, we should assume that the reading hands advantage helps you more than it does them.

The First Level

In many tournaments the first level is at very small stakes compared to the buy-in. This is especially true in the larger tournaments where players may have come a long distance to play. Tournament organizers like to make sure that those players have almost no chance of busting out early, so at the very least they get a few hours of play for their money. Since your results in the first level of tournaments like these, are almost inconsequential to your eventual chances of winning, you may want to consider playing much looser than you will in succeeding levels. This is especially true if you don't expect your table to be broken up for awhile.

The reason, of course, is that you are trying to create an impression you can take advantage of when the stakes rise. I have already mentioned that in limit tournaments your early tight, timid play will allow you to steal pots later on as the stakes go up. On the other hand, timid play might cost you a bit of money. One way to alleviate that problem is by playing rather loose during the first level only. Then, during the second and third level you revert to the tighter play, while from the fourth level on you would typically continue to play tight, but make more frequent aggressive stabs at stealable pots.

Hourly Rate Considerations

Suppose you were playing a $1,000 freezeout heads-up match against a truly awful player. Because he plays so terribly, you can almost guarantee yourself a win by grinding him out, and taking no chances. You might be able to steal lots of antes, get him to call you on the end when he has no chance, and do other things to almost ensure a win. Because of that, you choose to stay away from big pots where you are only a small favorite. For instance, you wouldn't put in a lot of money on fourth street when playing stud, even if your first four cards were a four-card straight flush.

By playing this way, you estimate that you have a 90 percent chance of winning the freezeout. That means that this freezeout is worth $800 to you in expected value.

$$\$800 = (.90)(\$1,000) - (.10)(\$1,000)$$

(If you played it 10 times, you expect to be ahead $8,000.) If the average number of hours this freezeout took was five, your expected hourly rate would be $160 per hour.

$$\$160 = \frac{\$800}{5}$$

What if you chose to gamble it up with him, pushing small edges and generally playing bigger pots? Suppose you estimated that this strategy reduced your chances of winning the freezeout to 75 percent? But suppose that playing this way meant the typical freezeout only took two hours, as opposed to five? Your expected earn per freezeout has gone down to $500.

$$\$500 = (.75)(\$1,000) - (.25)(\$1,000)$$

but your hourly rate has increased to $250.

$$\$250 = \frac{\$500}{2}$$

So which way should you play?

There is no definitive answer. It depends on a few different things, the most important of which is, what are those saved hours worth to you? If you would have spent them idly, you probably would prefer to make more money at a lower hourly rate. Most people, if offered the opportunity to make $800 in five hours, or $500 in two hours, would choose the former, as long as the job was not too taxing. Unless you are quite wealthy it would be hard to justify giving up $300 merely to gain three hours of leisure.

On the other hand, if you had an opportunity to make money during those three hours, the situation is different. For instance, if someone was willing to pay you $150 an hour to babysit during those three hours, you should, in theory, play the shorter freezeout, earn your $500 in expected value, and then pick up another $450 from your babysitting job. That $950 is better than the $800 you would theoretically earn if you played the long, drawn out way.

Another time that you would opt to play the shorter, though less profitable freezeout, would be when you knew that you could play more than one freezeout with this guy. If he is willing to play you 10 hours a day, playing as many $1,000 freezeouts as he can fit in, you would make a lot more EV wise ($2,500 versus $1,600) by opting to gamble. (You also would be more likely to keep him coming back, since he would quit sooner if you were winning 90 percent of the matches.)

There is, however, one other possible reason to play the more conservative style: Namely, your bank roll. If you only have a few thousand dollars to your name, winning the freezeout is too important to take chances, and this is the situation for most people who play tournaments. Unless there is a juicy sidegame, or perhaps a juicy evening satellite tournament that you know you could get into if you go broke early in the tournament, there is little reason to be concerned about your hourly rate when playing tournaments.

If George makes $100,000 a year in 200 tournaments where he is actually sitting at the table 1,000 hours, he has made $100 an hour. If Jane, playing the same 200 tournaments, has sat at the table 1,500 hours, and made $120,000, she has earned only $80 an hour. But most would prefer Jane's results over George's. The strategies recommended in this book assume that you would too. And it is yet another reason why avoiding slightly positive EV situations that can get you broke is usually the right thing to do.

Limping

When discussing the Gap Concept, we were assuming that the opener, whether it be you or someone else, brought it in for a raise. In that case we learned that good tournament strategy usually means a large gap between what you would raise with, and what you would call (or reraise) with. But what about merely calling to open? Should you ever do that? And what if they merely call? Poker players have a name for this type of opening. They call it "limping."

In general, you should rarely limp in a limit hold 'em tournament. There is simply too great a chance that you will steal the blinds with a raise. You give up that chance when you limp. Those hands that you might limp in with in a ring game in hopes of getting multiway action, now do better with a raise, if they are played at all. Because multi player pots are much rarer in tournaments. Thus, hands like

or

under the gun, if played at all, should usually be brought in with a raise.

Remember, however, we are speaking of limit rather than no-limit. It's also a little different for Omaha high-low-split eight-or-better, or seven-card stud. Since it is rare to steal the blinds in Omaha high-low-split eight-or-better, even in a tournament, you may choose to limp with some hands in early position, just as you would in a sidegame. I won't go into which hands those are, because this is not a book on poker strategy. For those who are interested in Omaha high-low-split eight-or-better, I suggest *High-Low-Split Poker for Advanced Players* by Ray Zee.

Playing seven-card stud tournaments, you will limp fairly often, just as you would in a sidegame. The difference between seven-card stud and hold'em, is that one of your cards is showing. Because of that you cannot as easily represent a powerful hand when your upcard is small, and thus have little chance of an ante steal in those situations. The most obvious example of when you should probably limp, is when you have a live three flush with a small card showing such as

If, however, your three flush was with a high upcard such as and no one else is yet in, you revert back to the Gap Concept, and would raise with this hand more than you would in a sidegame, knowing that the chances of winning right there have increased. (Notice that the two sample hands above each contain the same three cards. But the first one has the 4♥ up, and the second one has the J♥ in the door.)

Getting back to mainly hold 'em, what if someone limps in front of you? Because it is a tournament, even limpers will tend to be tighter than they would be in sidegames. Therefore, you should also be more selective. If your hand is merely good, you should be more apt to simply limp behind them rather than raise. In fact, you would generally need a better hand to limp behind a limper than you would need to raise with if no one was yet in. To raise that limper, you need a better hand yet.

In a hold 'em tournament, if a good player limped in first position, and I was in middle position, I would usually fold

(but call if the hand was suited), and call with

In stud, if a small card limped in I would not usually raise without a big pair even though in a sidegame I would often raise with a

hand like

No-limit hold 'em is different. The best players should be doing a lot of limping, even with mediocre hands. The Gap Concept doesn't apply (preflop) in the early rounds where the stack size is great compared to the blinds.

Actually, the Gap Concept only kicks in on later rounds in the early stages of a no-limit hold 'em tournament. On the later rounds you can make a lot of plays at the pot without very much, but quickly give up with pretty good hands if someone else is betting. Before the flop, however, implied odds and superior skill allow you to limp with lots of hands with decent prospects, whether or not players have limped in front of you.

When Will
Your Table Break Up?

One difference between a tournament and a sidegame is that after a while, due to the combining of tables as people go broke, you will often find yourself against completely different opponents.[6] This has implications to your strategy, especially if you have some idea when your table will break up. (Many tournaments have a preordained set order for breaking tables. Sometimes this order is announced to everyone, and sometimes it isn't. If nothing has been announced, you should try to find out for yourself by asking a tournament director what the plans are regarding the future breaking up of your table.)

If it looks like your table will break up soon, that has two possible effects on your strategy. The obvious one is that you make no "advertising" plays, since you will probably not have time to reap the benefits. Don't make an ill conceived bluff in hopes of eliciting calls later on. Don't play extra timidly to try and set up a bluff in the future. The people you are trying to set up won't be in your game in a few minutes.

The other time you might change your strategy if your table is scheduled to break up soon, is when you are playing against much tougher opponents than the average player in the rest of the room. When you are at a table like that, it would be a shame to go broke, or near broke when a much easier table is soon coming along. This is yet another example of a tournament situation

---

[6] In major tournaments there is sometimes a complete redraw for seats. This usually occurs when tournaments extend to a second day. All remaining players come back that next day to new seats. There is also frequently a redraw when the tournament reaches the final two or three tables.

where you might choose to pass up a small edge that could backfire, thus keep you from taking advantage of a larger edge in the future. This principle is especially true if you are playing no-limit or pot-limit. If your tough table will be soon broken up, stay away from close gambles.

(When I say soon broken up, I would typically mean within an hour or two. But it depends on your stack and how fast the stakes are going up. You may not have time to wait that long, and will have to gamble with your chips if you do. On the other hand, sometimes you can wait even longer. The first day of the $10,000 No-Limit Hold 'em World Championship at the World Series of Poker, the blinds start out so small and move up so slowly that few tables are broken up at all that day. The second day, however, everyone redraws for seats. In this tournament, when my initial table is extra tough, I am willing to wait out the whole day and be content to bring my $10,000 buy-in up to $15,000 or $20,000, rather than risk going broke and missing my chance to play against worse players the second day.)

If it is obvious that you will have to play at a table for a long time, your strategy switches from the above. Setting up plays for the future are even more important to do than in regular sidegames. Your opponents will be exactly the same, and the play you set up will be most likely at bigger stakes than the original play you used to start the process. If you find yourself at a tough table that will not break up, you have to make the best of it. You can't play extra tightly in the hopes of conserving your chips for a different table. You must simply accept that you are in trouble if you get worse than average cards, and therefore, play in such a way that will win you some chips if you do get lucky.

Adjusting Strategy
Because the Stakes Rise

Is there any reason to adjust strategy because the stakes rise every hour or so? There may very well be, but not in the way you may think. I have often heard it said that, if your stack is short, you must take chances *now* because you will not have enough chips to play with once the stakes go up. That is totally wrong. In fact, if anything, the reverse is true.

One time this is obvious is near the end of the tournament where your short stack is a bit smaller than some opponents. At the present stakes your opponent has more than enough chips to avoid going broke on one hand. But at the next level, he doesn't. If the stakes will soon rise, you should avoid taking risks in marginal situations at the lower limit, since there is a better chance you will be able to sneak into a higher money position at the higher stakes where the stacks that are slightly ahead of you are apt to bust out. Put another way, once the stakes are increased, those opponents who have a small chip lead over you have less of an edge since all of you are now in a position of risking going broke if you play a hand to the river. So that is a reason you would actually play a little tighter until the stakes are raised, to try to get into that position.

Here's an example. Suppose you are playing limit hold 'em and have reached the money. The stakes are now $100-$200. If there is betting on every round it can cost you at least $600 (in tournament chips). ($100 before the flop, $100 on the flop, $200 on the turn, and $200 on the river.) So, if you have less than that and one of your opponents has a little more, perhaps $800, you may want to play a little tighter than normal if the stakes will soon be raised.

57

Let's say you do this, the stakes are doubled, and your chip positions haven't changed. Now you need at least $1,200 to play a hand to the river. But notice that the advantage the $800 chip holder has over you has been reduced, for now, unlike before, he cannot complete a hand and still have chips left if there has been betting all the way through.

Another reason to consider playing a bit tighter before the stakes rise has to do with one of your superior skills. This might sound strange, because in general skillful players lose some of their advantage as their chips go down. But this can reverse when that player's stack is very small. The reason is that superior players are well versed in the value of various hands in all-in situations. Most tournament players, however, are rather inept at knowing what to do when they or their opponent might be going all-in early in the hand. So if you happen to have a stack that is a little bit bigger than what would be required to move in early, you may be better off waiting to the next raise in stakes, so that the same size stack becomes an all-in stack.[7]

The biggest reason, however, to change your strategy because of subsequent increases in stakes, are that the payoffs from creating an impression early are greater than they would be in a normal game. This can work in two different ways. You could play somewhat aggressively, or even wildly early on, in the hopes that it is noticed, and that this results in getting calls down the road that you otherwise might not have gotten when you have a big hand. That strategy pays off more in tournaments than it does in a normal game because those calls will be at bigger stakes.

The alternate strategy would be to play very tightly, and even timidly early on, in order to set up a bluff down the road. Again, this works better in a tournament than in a normal game because the pot you steal will be bigger given the raised stakes, in

---

[7] See the chapter entitled "All-in Strategy" for more discussion.

comparison to the loss of equity that you sustain by playing less than optimally at the smaller stakes.

So which of these two alternate strategies should you use? Obviously you usually can't use both in the same tournament. As a general rule, the answer would be that you should use the first strategy in no-limit or pot-limit tournaments, and the second strategy in limit tournaments. This is pretty much common sense, although I don't think it is a hard and fast rule. It especially may be true that the second strategy, of playing timidly at first to set up bluffs later, might be the preferred one even in no-limit or pot-limit tournaments.

Of course, the above two strategies should not be used if you believe your table will be breaking up soon. (See the chapter entitled "When Will Your Table Break Up?")

Noticing The Short Stacks

The idea that you should alter your play in the tournament depending on how many chips your opponents have in front of them is probably a bit over-rated. Some tournament players make rather drastic adjustments depending on their stack compared to others. They go too far with this idea, especially in the early stages. That being said, there are in fact, some adjustments that should be made.

Even putting aside strategy for the last table, it is important to pay attention to who is on a short stack. Typically, players with much less than the average amount of chips in front of them are ready to give up — hopefully you don't fall in that category. Because of that tendency, it is often unwise to make your usual semi-bluff thrust at a small pot. That play works well when players are anxious to conserve their chips. Small stacks, early in a tournament, are not thinking this way, and will be much more likely to call. (The same is almost as true for most players with large stacks. So you stay away from your normally aggressive opening style when your opponents are not mainly moderate stacks.)

Another reason to notice whether you might be up against a short stack is so that you can adjust your hand selection towards starting hands that do well "hot and cold."[8] This concept applies mainly to hold 'em, especially no-limit hold 'em, where putting your opponent all-in before the flop means the value of hands are shifted. For example,

---

[8] Hot and cold means that you are dealing out all the cards with no betting.

is normally much better than

but not if you are running the cards out against the kinds of hands (such as king-ten or king-nine) that a desperate short stack might call you with.

There is a situation where some players pay too much attention to short stacks, in spite of what you may have heard. Many so called experts advocate going much too far out of your way to eliminate players. For instance, in a multiway pot with one person all-in, they suggest "checking it down" with your other opponents who still have money, unless your hand is far superior. The idea is that by playing this way you will have increased the chances of busting the short stack because you don't drive out others. They also advocate getting all-in against a short stack, rather than leaving him with a few chips, even with hands that might not seem worth it. The idea again being that by playing this way you will guarantee his elimination when you do win the pot.

Both of these ideas are usually wrong. The only time they have some merit is at the very end of the tournament. And even then, only when you have a moderately small stack yourself. In those cases, his elimination can add quite a bit to your EV, which might indicate that you play less than what would normally be optimal, in order to increase the chances of that elimination. Aside from that one exception, however, you should not make sub-optimal plays simply because it might help eliminate that short stack. (Be glad others are doing that though.) You yourself adjust to short stacks only because you can assume they are getting desperate, and because hands that you play against them will not involve a bet on every round.

Noticing The Large Stacks

It is also important to notice those players who have large stacks. Most players in this situation have lost their fear of going broke, and are more likely both to call you with mediocre holdings, or initiate the betting with such holdings. In other words, they tend to play looser than the moderate stacks. The Gap, discussed earlier, narrows against them. You need to loosen up slightly when they open the pot, and tighten up slightly when they are behind you and you are considering opening.

This advice, of course, is a generalization. There are some players who remain quite cautious, even with a large stack. (Likewise, for some players with a short stack.) You should definitely keep your eyes out for these players who don't fit the norm, and adjust accordingly.

When the
Blinds are Coming Up

Suppose there is only one hand to go before your blind and you have only enough chips to put in that blind when it comes to you. There are many people who say that you should play this first hand as long as it is better then your average hand. This, in spite of the fact that it may be much worse than the hand you would normally need to play in this position. Their reasoning is that you will be forced to play an average hand (on average) your next hand, (when you are in the blind), so anything better than that would be preferable to play now.

Others reject that concept and suggest you do not alter your strategy simply because you will soon be forced to go all-in or near all-in on your blind. So who's right?

The answer is neither one. It turns out that in situations like this you should play hands worse than normal, but not merely better than average. It is somewhere in between.

Remember earlier we showed mathematically that if tomorrow you have an opportunity to make a great bet for a certain fixed amount of money, you should pass up merely good bets today if losing them will keep you from making that great bet tomorrow. With similar math we can show that the converse is also true. If you are forced to make a terrible bet tomorrow, it strangely enough, becomes right to make a merely bad bet today, if losing that bet allows you to skip tomorrow's bet. This is true, even if losing that first bet means you are broke.

For instance, if tomorrow you were forced to make an even money bet of $100, on a 20 percent shot, you should make an earlier $100 bet on as little as a 28.57 percent shot, if losing that bet means you don't bet tomorrow. Notice, however, you should not bet if you are below 28.57 percent. It is not correct to take a bad bet now to avoid an even worse bet later, if today's bet is almost as bad.

These mathematical results can be applied to the tournament situation where you are about to go close to all-in on your big blind (or in stud where you are down to your very last few antes). If you have one hand left, you need a hand that is somewhat better than your average hand to play. It cannot merely be slightly better. For instance, in hold 'em, depending on the number of players sitting at the table

is about an average hand, and so is

With one hand to go at a full table, you should not play Q♠8♥ or Q♠5♠.[9] I would estimate you would need something along the lines of king-nine offsuit, queen-ten offsuit, or jack-eight suited.

If there is more than one hand to go before you are forced to put in the blind or your final ante, the degree you loosen up compared to how you would play if you could quit without taking your blind, would be less. Once you get to the point where you

---

[9] It should be noted that Q♠8♥ is a more than slightly better hand than Q♠7♥ due to the fact that Q♠8♥ can use both of its cards to make a straight while Q♠7♥ cannot.

can still wait four or five hands, there should be almost no change in your strategy as compared to normal. Notice, however, that when I refer to your normal strategy, I am not speaking of your strategy with lots of chips. Rather, I am speaking of normal all-in strategy (where you are not forced to play your upcoming blind short-stacked).

To show what I mean by this let's take the hand

under the gun. There are many games where, with lots of chips in front of you, it is correct to limp. On the other hand, if you only have the amount of the big blind, you should fold if you were planning to quit after this hand. However, if instead, you are required to play the big blind if you fold (as you would be in a tournament) you should again call with this hand.

All-In Strategy

Though I have rarely seen it mentioned elsewhere, one of the major differences between regular poker games and tournament poker, is that in the tournaments a player is often all-in.[10] The correct strategy involving all-in decisions is usually the same for both sidegames and tournaments. However, these situations come up so infrequently in a sidegame that the knowledge concerning how to play them is not needed to be a successful sidegame player. That is not the case in tournaments.

Notice that you need to understand all-in concepts, not only because you will often be a short stack, but also because you will often be *against* a short stack. Either way there will be no further betting on later rounds, so you must know which hands to choose to play in these situations.

Before going into some specifics, I want to mention an important point regarding being all-in. That point is that it is actually to your advantage to be out of chips, especially if it is early in a hand. This might seem intuitively wrong, particularly if you are a very good player, because your weapons (namely your chips) have been taken away from you. All you can do is helplessly watch the cards come off and hope your hand wins. However, in spite of the fact that being all-in keeps you from using your skill, this is more than made up for, on average, by the fact that you are guaranteed to see the last card.

To give an extreme example, suppose you are playing seven-card stud and are all-in for the ante. If you are playing in an eight handed game you would win one out of eight pots if everyone went to the river. But since many of the players are folding, you will sometimes win pots that otherwise would have been won by

---

[10] If you don't know what that means, you are not ready for this book.

one of those players who threw their hand away. Depending on how players play, you might win one in five of those pots you were all-in. Thus you would be getting 7-to-1 odds on a 4-to-1 shot. If you were playing $30-$60 with a $5 ante, your expected profit would be $3.00.

$$\$3 = \left(\frac{1}{5}\right)(7)(\$5) - \left(\frac{4}{5}\right)(\$5)$$

If you could do this every hand, you would make about $100 an hour, which is much more than even great players make with lots of chips in front of them.

Because being all-in is so advantageous, the advice you often hear, to start playing poor hands when your stack is short, since you no longer have time to wait for a good hand, is for the most part wrong (except in extreme situations discussed in the previous chapter). There is no reason to play much weaker hands to avoid going all-in soon thereafter. Even if you throw all your hands away until that one last hand, where you are forced all-in, it is not so terrible. To give up sooner than that, and play a very bad hand is a big mistake.

The subject of all-in play is quite complex, especially when more than two people are involved. Even if only heads-up situations are considered, there are so many different possibilities that could be mathematically analyzed as to allow a whole book to be written about it. In this chapter I will merely outline some basic situations and what needs to be considered in those situations. Those who want to know the subject in more detail will have to delve into it themselves.

Basically there are four heads-up situations that could result in an all-in pot:

1. You are the short stack and the aggressor.
2. You are the short stack and the defender.
3. You are the larger stack and the aggressor. And,

4.   You are the larger stack and the defender.

Let us examine these one by one. (These situations are more clear cut in hold 'em than in seven-card stud or Omaha high-low-split eight-or-better, so I will use hold 'em for my examples. Those who are playing other games will have to extrapolate.)

Suppose you are playing limit hold 'em and are in the big blind, and all you have left is just enough to call a raise. All fold to the small blind, who raises without looking at his cards. You have

Should you call?

What we have here is a pure math problem. In fact, almost all of these all-in situations are pure math problems. That should be obvious since there is no further betting and no further skill. Anyway, in this particular case the answer is definitely yes. Why? Because a trey-deuce has (coincidentally) a 32 percent chance of beating two random cards, and you are getting 3-to-1 on this call.[11]

The reason I know that trey-deuce has a 32 percent chance is because I own a computer program that will let you punch in one hand against another or one specified hand against one random hand. Serious tournament players must purchase one of these programs.

The example I gave was rather simple. We knew his hand was random because he never looked at his cards, and you had exactly enough money to call his raise. I can tell you right now

---

[11] Trey-deuce is the worst possible hand played against two random cards "hot and cold," i.e. no betting.

that in this specific situation, (i.e. you are in the big blind) where a player is either raising in the dark or is in a strategic situation where he will raise with just about anything, you must call no matter what you have. (There is one possible exception. If you throw your hand away here and then throw the next hand away also, you will have half a big blind in front of you that could conceivably be enough to move you up in the standings. Thus, if one or more players besides you have tiny stacks and figure to go broke when the blind comes to them, you would fold many hands, so you could squeak into a higher money position.) You are getting at least 3-to-1 odds and no two cards are that much of an underdog to a random or near random hand.

It gets a lot more ticklish, however, if

1.   You have more than enough to call.
2.   It is a no-limit hand where his raise gives you less than 3-to-1 odds to call. Or,
3.   The hand you are facing is to varying degrees better than random.

Suppose the big blind was $100 (in tournament chips), the small blind was $50, you had another $200 in chips, and the small blind again raised in the dark. Since we can assume that the small blind will probably bet any flop and that you are often forced to call (getting 5-to-1 odds at this point), the true or effective odds you are getting before the flop are not 300-to-100 but are in fact 400-to-200. This makes calls with your absolute worst hands more borderline.

If you are playing no-limit, the size of your opponent's raise now becomes very relevant. Thus, even if you think he will raise with anything, you should still throw away your worst hands when his raise will put you all-in and give you odds of 2-to-1 or worse. So if you are in a $100 blind, have $400 or more in front of you, and your opponent moves you in, you are getting $600-to-$400 odds (or 3-to-2). And even if his hand is random, you can't call unless you have something along the lines of

since this hand will win a little better than 40 percent of the time against a random holding.

Suppose you have some inkling about what type of hands your opponent will raise you with. If that is the case, you can, in theory, calculate which hands to call with based on his possible holdings and the odds you are getting. In order to do this well you have to have done some research away from the table using one of these computer programs along with some combinatorics.

To give an overly simplified example, suppose you were in the big blind with $100 and held

Your opponent in the small blind attempted to move you in with a $600 bet (thus giving you 7-to-5 odds), and you put your opponent on aces, kings or ace-king. Two jacks is in big trouble against two out of three of those hands. To make the call right, the jacks must win more than 41 percent of the time. But it is too simplistic to say that the jacks are in trouble two out of three times and you should fold. That is because the aces and kings are dealt less often than ace-king. On the other hand, the aces and kings are bigger favorites over jacks than jacks are over ace-king.

To get the answer you must do some calculating. First you must realize that a pair of aces can be dealt in six different ways. Ditto for the kings. Ace-king, on the other hand, can be dealt in 16 different ways. Meanwhile, when the jacks are facing one of the 12 combinations of aces or kings, they will win only about 2 of those 12 times. Against the ace-king, they will win about 9 of the 16 times. Altogether, therefore, they will win 11 out of 28 times.

$$11 = 2 + 9$$

$$28 = 12 + 16$$

That is 39.3 percent or just a tad short of the required 41.67 percent.

$$39.3 = (100)\left(\frac{11}{28}\right)$$

Thus, the proper play is probably to fold. Notice, however, that a slightly smaller raise or the inclusion of ace-queen as a possible opposing hand would turn that fold into a call. As you can see, this type of calculation becomes, at best, only an estimate in the majority of situations. (By the way, if you do try to do this, you must take into account your own cards. So in the example given, if ace-jack was yet another hand that he might have, you need to realize that can only be dealt 8 ways rather than 16 because of the two jacks in your hand.)

To summarize the above, and how you could do it yourself with the aid of a computer, what you do is this: Enter your hand into the computer and run it against the possible hands that you think he could have. Let's say there were four different such hands. You will get 4 different percentages as to your chances of winning. But you cannot simply average them. That is because some of his hands will be dealt more often than others. You need to know how to count the number of combinations of the various hands he could have, including making the adjustment, when necessary, for the cards in your own hand. Armed with this information, you now take a *weighted* average of the four numbers the computer spit out, and compare that to the odds you are getting. How to calculate card combinations and take weighted averages is addressed in any good statistics or gambling book.

As difficult as these calculations are, they become even more difficult when you, as the short stack, are considering a raise yourself. This is different from when you are considering calling because you usually have a chance of winning the pot with your raise, unchallenged. Even when you know you will get called, the calculation is a bit different, so let's do that first.

Suppose you are on the button, have $200 left, no one else is in yet, the $50 small blind is throwing his hand away out of turn (to simplify things), and you know the big blind is a good player. Because he is a good player a raise on your part will almost certainly be called as he is getting 3½- to-1 odds. Knowing he will call, how good a hand do you need to raise with? We will assume that merely limping is not an option. *You* are getting $250-to-$200 (or 5-to-4) odds when you raise. Remember, he will always call you. That means you must win 200 out of 450 hands to have a positive EV. Therefore, you need to remember which hands have better than a 44½ percent chance of winning against a random hand; and raise with them, and throw away the others.

Let's say instead you had $500 on the button and were trying to figure out whether a raise would be profitable. This is not so easy to do. If you knew he would call you every time, it would be simple enough because getting $550-to-$500 odds, it is a simple matter to see which hands win often enough to make the play profitable. (Except for one very important thing. A profitable play is not necessarily the right play. That is because there may be another alternative which is even more profitable. In this case, where you know you will be called, it might well be better to merely limp with mediocre hands, since that might show a greater long run profit than raising with them.)

But because he will fold many of his hands, you need to break things down. When he folds you win $150. Since your raise costs you $500 it would show a small profit (of $7) if it steals the pot 78 percent of the time, even if you never won those times that you were called.

$$\$7 = (.78)(\$150) - (.22)(\$500)$$

But of course you will win many of the times you are called, which means that you need not succeed in your steal anywhere near that often to make the play right. For instance, suppose you thought that he will fold half the time if you make that $500 raise. How often would you need to win those other times (when he called you) to make the overall play profitable?

I will not bore you with the algebra required to do this problem. Instead, let us throw out a number and see whether it would be enough. Suppose you stole the ante 50 percent of the time and won 30 percent of the remaining showdowns. That means that in twenty hands you would have won $150 ten times, won $550 three times, and lost $500 seven times. Your total win would be $3,150 and your total loss is $3,500.

$$\$3,150 = (10)(\$150) + (3)(\$550)$$

$$-\$3,500 = (7)(-\$500)$$

In this particular case the play would not be quite worth it. If you stole the pot slightly more often, or won the pot slightly more often when you didn't steal, this play would swing to a positive one. Again, however, remember that it doesn't mean it is the right play if an alternative play is still yet more positive.

Anyway, the break even point for the above problem, assuming he will throw his hand away half the time, is that you need to win one-third of the those times he doesn't throw his hand away. Armed with this information and a lot of patience, we can figure out about what hands are raising hands. We know about what hands he will fold, since we know he will throw half his hands away. The question now becomes, given he has a calling hand, what hands of ours will win one-third of the time, weighted average wise, against those hands?

Clearly a hand like 3♣2♥ is not one of them. It only wins 32 percent of the time against a random hand. But even hands that win 35 percent against a random hand are apt to win less than the required 33 percent against the hands that he will call with. As you can see, finding the precise answers to these questions is almost impossible. But making estimates, now that you see what is entailed, should be within your grasp.

When you have the larger stack, and a smaller stack moves in against you, it is again a math question, once you have used your judgment to determine the possible hands he will make that play with. You see what odds you are getting, you look at your hand, and you estimate his possible hands. You take the weighted average of your chances with each of those possible hands and see whether your pot odds makes the call worth it. Of course, this assumes that everyone else has already folded. If there are still players yet to act, or if other players have already called, you would need to increase the strength of your hand, perhaps significantly, before you would make this call.

If you are a larger stack that is contemplating putting a small stack all-in, the math is the same as it was above, where you combine your chances of stealing the pot with your chances of winning if you are called. Again this assumes that other players are out or are quite likely to be out. The difference, however, is that when you are making this play against a short stack, there is a wide range of possibilities as far as what his calling proclivities might be.

Depending on the player and the tournament situation at the time, you may be looking at a circumstance where you figure him to throw away 90 percent of his hands. If so, a moderate raise with any two cards is the right play. At other times, the short stack may be desperate, or have given up to the point where you can expect a call the majority of the time. In such cases you would need a much better hand to make this raising play.

As you can see, there is a lot to consider when hands will be played all-in. There are, however, some simple rules of thumb. In hold 'em, you should realize that certain hands go up or down in value depending on whether there will be future betting. A hand like

is rarely worth playing all-in, whereas

or

may well be worth moving in with, even though they should usually be folded if more chips are at risk later.

In the case of seven-card stud, if an all-in pot seems imminent, small and medium pairs go up in value, while small three flushes and three straights go down. So you might play a hand like

but throw away a hand like

In Omaha high-low-split eight-or-better, a hand like

is probably worth playing all-in, even in spots where it would normally be folded.

Just Out of The Money

The following advice assumes that there is a decent pay off for the lowest money prize. That lowest prize might be offered to the ninth place or eighteenth place in a hold 'em tournament, or eighth place or sixteenth place in a stud tournament.

Let's say everyone at the last two tables gets paid, with last place being 2 percent of the total prize pool. Suppose there are three tables left, where one or two players need to go broke before they combine into the last two tables. Should you alter your strategy because of this situation?

Well, if you have a lot of chips, you certainly should. In the next chapter, the special last two table situation is addressed where I point out how advantageous it is to be one of the chip leaders who can steal from those short stacks that are trying to sneak into the money. This really is a profitable situation. Even when you are a medium stack you can take a little advantage of it those times that the larger stacks are already out.

But what if you are one of the short stacks? Should you alter your play to try to sneak into the money? Let me stop here and make one point. Though there will be times when your overall tournament mathematical expectation can be increased by folding hands that are normally slightly profitable, you may not want to. Because by doing so, you have turned a small chance of getting a major prize into a tiny chance. This might be unpalatable to you in spite of the minor increase in EV. Given the small amount of money involved, I have no problem with anyone who chooses to make absolutely no adjustments with their short stacks rather than try to sneak into the money. In the long run, they will make slightly less than those who look only at their EV, and they will much more often get the "booby prize" of coming in one out of the money. On the other hand, they will probably slightly increase their chances to reach one of the higher prizes, which for some people is an extra reward in itself.

If, however, you are concerned about getting into the money, there are things you can do to help yourself. One of the main things is to physically get up from your table and notice how your stack compares to everyone else's, not just those at your table. You might have the lowest stack at your table, (which would mean that you may as well gamble if it was the last table), but your stack is bigger than the stack of one or two players at the other tables. Assuming we are talking about stacks that are so small that losing one hand will deplete it completely, you should stay away from all close gambles, and maybe even some not so close gambles, (e.g. calling an early raiser with

in hold 'em), if it looks like that will significantly increase your chances of getting into the money.

This situation occurs when there are some stacks smaller than yours. It also occurs when you have the smallest stack, as long as you don't think the other small stacks are going out of their way waiting for you to go broke. (If it does look like they are waiting you out, and your stack is smallest, you should play no tighter than you normally would in this situation.)

A Special Last
Two Table Situation

Suppose there are only two tables left, with five players at each table. If one more player goes broke, the tables are combined. The tournament pays nine places. At this point all of the short stacks are desperately trying to survive.

The difference between tenth place and ninth place is usually pretty significant (when the last table starts with nine players), even when tenth place pays a nominal amount. With the combination of the two tables imminent, these short stacks will tend to throw away all but their very best hands rather than risk the booby prize (coming in 10th). Because of that, the chip leader at both tables is in a wonderful position, especially in games with blinds. When no one has yet opened, he can raise with an awful lot of hands since his chances of stealing the pot are so high. (The player with the second largest stack at each table is in a similar position if the largest stack has already folded, as long as that second largest stack is also pretty big.)

It is not uncommon for the largest stack at each of the two five handed tables to significantly increase his chip position during this time, even without ever playing a hand to the river. He merely steals the blinds hand after hand.

In addition, because of this syndrome, the chip leader at each table has an opportunity to make a very unusual strategy adjustment. Suppose he is on the button with:

80

and the player with the shortest stack raises, almost all-in. *The two queens should probably fold!* Do you see why? The gain from playing this hand, perhaps a small bet in expected value, is not worth the fact that if you do win the pot, the tables are combined, and you can no longer run over the game.

This of course is a rather unique situation to be in, so knowing it will not help your long term tournament results very much. I bring it up more to show how the nature of tournaments is such that they can occasionally indicate a strategy far different from what you are used to.

The Last Table

In almost all tournaments, reaching the last table means getting into the money. In some cases, significant money. Ninth place at the $10,000 No-Limit Hold 'em Championship at the World Series of Poker is over $50,000. And each higher place adds that much more money. Because the amount involved in moving up a place or two can be significantly more than the face value of your chips, it is almost mandatory that you take this into account if the money is important to you.

(If winning the tournament is really your only goal, more power to you. You would then not make most of the strategy adjustments that I am about to recommend when your chips are low. Just realize that you are sacrificing a lot of EV in your quest to win.)

On the other hand, many tournament players go too far trying to move up the ladder. They actually lose EV with their strategy that places too much emphasis on surviving in hopes of finishing a bit higher. The only justification for what they do would be if their bankroll was such that the extra money they often win is so important to them that it is worth *badly* hurting their chances of getting a top prize.

The strategy adjustments for the last table designed to move you up in the standings really only apply to the players with fairly short stacks. If you have a moderate stack, you should make few adjustments. For instance, if their are nine players left, and you have an average amount of chips, and are in about fifth place, you could almost certainly ante your way into getting sixth prize. But given the typically giant increase in prizes paid to the last three places, any strategy along those lines (anteing your money off) would be ridiculous. Yes, you will sometimes wind up coming in seventh or eighth by playing your normal game, but you will far more often come in the top three as well. The upside of extreme caution when you have a moderate stack, is simply not worth the downside.

There is one major exception. It occurs when you are playing no-limit, and you are facing a stack that can bust you. Here you should probably not risk all your chips as a slight favorite, since a loss would bring you instantly down to ninth place. This would be especially true if doubling your chips would still not make you one of the leaders.

There are some tournaments in which the lesser prizes go up very slowly. Sometimes not at all. For instance, eighth and ninth place may pay the same. In tournaments like this, there should be virtually no change in your strategy with a short stack and nine players, regardless of your chip position. Significant strategic changes might not occur until there are six or seven players left.

Each tournament is different, so you will have to use your judgment to decide to what degree you would alter your strategy due to prize structure. But the basic idea is this: *If you are in next to last place, but still quite short, you should tend to go out of your way to avoid going broke before the shorter stack does.*

(The assumption is made that if you both continue to ante or blind off your money, he would go broke first. This is almost always the case in stud. [Barring a lot of unlucky bring-ins]. It may not be the case in hold 'em or Omaha. He could have slightly less than you, yet because the blinds will get to you first, you will go broke before he does if neither of you play a hand. In that case you should consider yourself as having the smaller stack.)

How far you take this depends on the exact chip situation. For instance, if there is $100,000 in total buy-ins, eight players left, the shortest stack has $1,000, you have $1,500, and the next player has $7,000, that would be different than if the three stacks were $4,000, $5,000, and $6,000, and you had the $5,000. In the first case, you have very little chance of moving into sixth place, no matter what you do. So if there is a significant difference between seventh and eighth, you should try as best you can to ensure seventh. That means throwing away all but the very best hands.

The second situation is different. If you see that the shortest stack of $4,000 is playing incredibly tight, you could match that tightness and again have a very good chance to come in seventh. But the cost is too high. With sixth place only $1,000 ahead of you, and with you possessing 5 percent of the total chips, anteing your money off to preserve seventh would be a shameful way to play. You could still easily come in sixth or higher, by playing normally. Let that $4,000 stack succeed in outlasting you once in awhile. Who cares about him? There is too much money to be won for you to give it all up, just to try to outlast him.

When you have the smallest stack, the situation is the opposite. You should usually gamble, or at least not play any tighter than normal. This is especially true if you have enough chips to give you an outside chance to get lucky and win a high prize. But even if you don't have that many chips, it is more likely than not that the player who has the second smallest stack is waiting for you to go broke. So there is no point in waiting yourself. You can't outlast him.

Sometimes, of course, you will find yourself against a player with a slightly larger stack, who for whatever reason, is disregarding you and still taking chances. Against him, you should often revert to the strategy of the second largest stack, play extra tightly, and hope to sneak ahead of him. This is even more true in no-limit or pot-limit tournaments, where you might get lucky enough to witness a confrontation between two of the bigger stacks, which will move you up the prize ladder.

Disregarding the above exception, the complete turnaround in strategy from the next to smallest stack to the smallest stack, can reap some unexpected benefits. I have sometimes found myself at the last table in a tournament, possessing the next to smallest stack, playing quite tightly, and making an impression on all of my opponents. But most of them simply assume that I am trying to last. Then, the lowest stack doubles up. At that point I have the shortest stack, and I immediately start raising with far more hands. And those opponents who are not aware of what we have just been discussing have no idea that I have just significantly loosened up my playing requirements, and thereby quickly throw away all but their best hands. This often allows me to steal my way back into next to last position, whence I go back into my cocoon until the shorter stack goes broke or doubles up yet again.

For example, in limit hold 'em if you're the second shortest, stack don't even consider playing

if three to the right of the button. But if the smallest stack doubles up to pass you, this becomes a raising hand if first in, especially if your recent play was very tight.

Down to Two Players

If you are lucky enough to be one of the last two players, it is important that you don't relax, savor your score, and play less than your best. However, the truth is that your best will usually only give you a slight advantage. That is because the stakes are so high compared to the number of chips in play.

In most tournaments the stakes move up faster than the number of players move down, so by the time it is heads-up, losing two or three pots in a row that go all the way to the river will certainly eliminate the shorter stack. Because of that, you may want to make a deal using the simple formula I outlined in the chapter on that subject.

If you don't make a deal, should you change your strategy from typical heads-up games because this is a tournament? It depends on your skill level compared to your opponent's. If you know he is better than you, you must be aggressive. Do not try to "box" with him. Instead, go for a knock-out punch. If you're the better player, you should play your normal game, except you should try to avoid playing big pots with close decisions. Again though, these recommendations will have only a minor impact on your chances. The only major mistake you could make, if you are not used to playing heads-up, is to play so tightly that you are destined to be ground down from ante steals.

When I won the "World Championship" of Draw Poker, I found myself playing heads-up against a man who would not call my opening pot-size bet unless he had a pair of sevens or better. That meant he was throwing away his hand two out of three times before the draw. I was getting even money on my opening bet. That meant it was correct for me to open with any five cards. The fact that he would call only a third of the time made my eventual victory such a certainty that I would have avoided playing a giant pot, even with four of a kind.

Actually, I did not open with every single hand because I was petrified that he would start to realize how wrong he was to fold small pairs. So, I gave him the ante once in awhile.

I tell you this story to illustrate the one catastrophic strategy that you might use if you are not accustomed to heads-up poker, and get down to the last two players. Any other reasonable strategy will find you winning this tournament with a probability close to your percentage of the total chips.

Three Illustrative Plays

Here are three examples of good tournament plays that would be debatable in a sidegame.

Example No. 1: Limit Hold 'em. You are in the big blind with

Three people limp in, the small blind folds, and you check. The flop is

Everyone checks. The next card is the

Everyone checks. The last card is the

This is a very good bluffing opportunity. You are risking one big bet to win four and a half small ones. You are getting a little bit better than 2-to-1. In a situation like this your chances of succeeding ought to be at least 40 percent.

The other players know that you might well have an eight and cautiously checked it on fourth street, or even have sandbagged with a jack. There does not seem to be enough money in the pot to try to keep you honest, especially in a tournament. Normally suspicious players who might call you in a sidegame, will throw away a hand like ace high or even two fives without a second thought. In general, stealing small pots on the last or next to last round, when it seems like your opponents are weak, is much more likely to be worth the risk in a tournament than in a sidegame.

Example No. 2: Razz (seven-card lowball). With four low cards behind you, you raise with a

A four calls you. All others fold. You catch a jack and he catches a queen. In a tournament you should usually check.

There is no chance that he will fold, and your edge is small enough that it is probably not worth pushing. A bet on your part hurts him, but probably hurts you as well. The gainers are the other players (especially late in the tournament). When you check, it makes it easy to fold on fifth street if he catches a small one and you catch a big one. It also may allow you to win without a fight if you catch something like a seven and he catches an eight. Remember that in tournaments, winning pots immediately, rather than having merely a good chance to win a bigger pot, is usually preferred when you are one of the best players.

I would caution, however, that you do not take this principle to too great an extreme. In the example given, had you caught a ten instead of a jack, you would be wrong to check.

Example No. 3: No-limit hold 'em — third level. Five people limp in before the flop. You are the big blind holding

 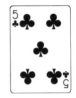

As long as nobody is near all-in, you should seriously consider a large raise. If, for instance, the blinds are $50 and $100, a $700 to $1,000 raise would be about right. Obviously if you are reraised you don't even think of calling (although you might pretend to think). This play is okay in a sidegame as well, as long as you don't do it too often, but is better yet in a tournament.

It is true that some players' starting hands will tend to be a bit better in tournaments than in sidegames, but it doesn't matter because they are still less likely to call a big raise if their hands are merely good. This is especially true if that big raise is a reasonable percentage of their stack.

In the example given I'm assuming that your raise is at least ten percent of your opponents' stacks. On the other hand, it should be less than 50 percent, otherwise someone may decide to go all-in with a mediocre hand, like

or

which would be a disaster for you.

This example brings up an important concept about no-limit hold 'em, both tournaments and sidegames. That concept is that if you raise in no-limit, especially before the flop, you should do it only when you don't mind a reraise.

But when I say "mind" I mean that in two possible different ways. You might not mind it because your hand is so good that you will welcome it, but you also might not mind it because you would have no misgivings about folding if you get reraised. That is obviously the situation with J♠5♣. Yet almost all players, except no-limit hold 'em experts, don't understand this. They are much more apt to make the play that I suggested with a hand like

or

That is very wrong. These are two hands that would very much mind being reraised. The reason of course, is that calling that reraise is very costly and probably incorrect, while folding means you missed out on decent chances to make a hand that might very well have won a big chunk from that reraiser or others.

So again, do not raise in no-limit hold 'em, especially tournaments, if there is a reasonable chance that a reraise will make you throw up.

Rebuy Tournaments

This book was written mainly to show you how to adjust from your normal winning strategies when you are playing in a poker tournament. But these new strategies assume that a player is eliminated when he goes broke. Some tournaments allow you to buy in again, after you go broke, at least during the first few hours. These are called "rebuy tournaments," and are quite common in the small buy-in, weekly tournaments. Even some events in the big tournaments, like the World Series of Poker, allow rebuys.

Besides letting you buy in two or more times when you go broke, many of these tournaments also allow you to "add-on" even if you are not broke. This option also expires after a few hours.

Because so many of your strategy changes in a tournament relate to the avoidance of being eliminated, (either yours or their's) much of what is in this book does not apply to rebuy tournaments *during the rebuy period.* Once that expires, however, the situation reverts back to normal, and the things we are learning here again apply. But now let us talk briefly about how you should play before the rebuy period expires, and whether you should rebuy.

In tournaments, where most people tend to rebuy if they go broke, your strategy during the rebuy period should somewhat revert back to that which you use in normal games. You would still, of course, adjust to any player who you notice is playing differently than usual ring game strategy. He may not be planning to rebuy, or is at least trying to avoid it. But it has been my experience that most players in a rebuy tournament play significantly looser before their rebuy option expires. This has obvious implications for your strategy. Most notably, it shrinks the "Gap" in your opening versus calling requirements.

By my saying that your initial strategy should be similar to normal sidegame strategy, you should deduce that I am assuming that you also will rebuy if *you* go broke. And, in fact, that is what I am assuming. If you are one of the better players in the tournament, how could that not be the right thing to do? Not only does your superior play make that second rebuy something with a positive EV, you also are taking advantage of the mathematical fact that smaller stacks are worth more per chip than the larger stacks, due to the prize structure.[12] (If you did not bring enough money to rebuy, you should tighten up even during the rebuy period. But not as much as you would tighten up if you were playing in a non-rebuy tournament, since your opponents are apt to be opening looser.)

What about adding on? Is this the right play even if you are not broke? The answer usually depends on how well you are doing. Basically, the more chips you have, the more you would be inclined not to add-on. The exact point at which adding on would be a bad play depends on many factors, such as prize structure, your skill level, how many players are left, and the size of your stack. I think a decent rule of thumb would be to add-on if you have less than the average number of chips at that point, and not otherwise.

There are two exceptions:

1.   A few tournaments allow add-ons far in excess of the original buy-in. If you can afford it, and are one of the best players, you must seriously consider making this add-on, even if you are already doing well.

2.   There are also some tournaments (not the major ones) that charge less per chip for your add-on than they do for your original buy-in. Again, you would have to almost always opt to purchase these cheaper chips.

Again, big money tournaments rarely offer rebuys. And even when they do, they turn into regular tournaments after two or three

---

[12] See the chapter entitled "Chips Change Value."

hours. That is why I have devoted only this short section to the subject. A more detailed analysis of the theory of rebuying can be found in *Poker Tournament Strategies* by Sylvester Suzuki.

Satellites

A satellite is a tournament to get into a tournament. For the high buy-in tournaments, satellites are big business. Most consist of one table. Occasionally, for very high buy-in tournaments, like the $10,000 No-Limit Hold 'em World Championship at the World Series of Poker, the satellites are often multi-table events called a Super Satellite.

There is no question that you can have an edge playing a satellite. I rarely play them because I can make more money hour rate wise by playing in the sidegames. However, it is a close decision, even for me, especially if I can pick and choose which satellite to play in. Often participants in satellites are much weaker than opponents in a normal game.

The proper strategy for a one table satellite is somewhere between the proper strategy for a regular tournament and a sidegame. Because there are not large prizes for second, third, and fourth, the idea of sneaking into those places does not arise. (Some one table satellites do have a small prize for second place, so on close decisions you might want to take that into account. But it is not a major aspect of your strategy.)

In theory, when there is only one winner, you should play exactly as if you were playing in a normal game. In practice, however, there are some adjustments even in a one table satellite compared to a sidegame. You still have to worry about the fact that you cannot buy more chips, and again we are presuming that you are just about the best player at the table. That means you should avoid gambling in close situations.[13] But they have to be very close because the short time duration of a satellite does not allow for your greater skill to make as much of a difference, and

---

[13] Again we are talking more about calling, not betting

therefore, you can't be throwing away most of your mildly profitable hands.

As far as taking advantage of the fact that your opponents don't want to go broke, I have found that many players in satellites really don't worry too much about it. It is important that you identify these players and contrast them with those who do worry. The idea, of course, is to determine which players to apply the Gap Concept against, and which ones not to.

The other aspect of a satellite that differs from a sidegame is again, the number of hands that will be played without enough chips to bet all the way to the river. Just as in normal tournaments, good satellite players must do some research to see how hands behave in a "hot and cold" manner in order to give them their best chance.

Super satellites are almost exactly the same as normal tournaments. In fact there is one type of super satellite that forces you to sometimes play even tighter than you would in normal tournament. I am speaking of super satellites where there are several winners, all of whom get the same prize, namely a buy-in for the big tournament. In that case, you could find yourself in a situation where it would be correct to throw every hand away, no matter what it was.

Suppose, for instance, the Super Satellite ended when there were five players left, each of whom would win a $10,000 buy-in. There are now seven players left and you are the chip leader. Three of the players are in imminent danger of going broke. What would you have to gain by playing even two aces? You are almost 100 percent guaranteed of winning your buy-in by doing nothing. Playing any hand gives you everything to lose with nothing to gain.

Super satellites often allow rebuys and add-ons. The principles involving the decision as to whether to rebuy or add-on are covered in the chapter on rebuy tournaments.

When All That
Matters is Winning

This book usually assumes that you are anxious to have as great an expected value in the tournament as possible. Because of the nature of the prize structure, the best way to accomplish this dictates a strategy that does not quite give you the best chance of winning the tournament.

This sacrifice is worth it though, because of the increased chances of getting into the money. But what if you don't care about the money? Suppose your goal is merely to have the greatest possible chance of winning it all. (There are a lot of good reasons why you might feel this way.) How many of the concepts in this book would still apply?

Actually, most still would. The Gap Concept, for instance, still applies, only slightly less strongly. Because it mainly relates to the other players' goals, not yours. You still will be raising with opening hands that are weaker than normal to take advantage of their propensity to fold. You will still be calling or reraising with hands that are stronger than normal because of their propensity to play tighter than normal (unless they themselves know the Gap Concept).

What about avoiding close gambles? This is not quite as true for you, when winning is your only goal. For instance you would not throw away the 54 percent shot in my mathematical example on page 36 in hopes of sneaking into a higher place. But earlier in the tournament you might very well still fold on a close decision, even if winning was your only goal.

The reason again is we are assuming you are one of the best players. So if a close decision involves a significant portion of your chips, you should avoid it, even if you don't care about the lesser prizes. You would prefer to preserve chips to let your skill have time to do its work.

One thing you might do differently is gamble in spots where only a small amount of chips are involved. For instance, you should find any excuse you can to play multiway pots, which if won, will allow you to amass many chips. You should gamble even more if you don't feel that you are one of the better players in the tournament, or if time means something to you.

To take an extreme example, suppose your heart is set on winning a World Series bracelet. You are short stacked with 12 players left. Sneaking into the money will mean coming back to play the last table the next day. That means you can't enter the next day's tournament. In such a case you might want to take major chances with 12 players so that you either move way up in chips or go broke, allowing you to play tomorrow.

Again, I have no problem with those of you who, for whatever reason, play this way to maximize your chances of winning the tournament. The EV you cost yourself is not that much. But it isn't insignificant either. As long as you realize that, fine.

Tournament Theory Afterthought

This section of the book showed how different tournaments can be from normal poker games. You are concerned with prize structure, chips changing value, and when your table will break up, among other things. These aren't even considerations in normal poker games.

Tournament differences impact how you should play your hands, they increase the "Gap," they force you to give up on many small edges, and frequently make overall play tighter.

All of this was illustrated in this section (and the preceding one), so it should now be obvious that even if you have a good understanding of poker strategy in general, but don't understand the appropriate tournament adjustments, your overall results will only be marginal at best. So I suggest that if you are really serious about playing tournament poker, that you reread this and the previous section as many times as is necessary, until you get it.

Part Three
Other Topics

Other Topics
Introduction

The following section deals with some disparate miscellaneous topics that relate to poker tournaments. Some involve playing strategy, some don't. But they are all important.

Last Longer Bets

It is a common practice among tournament players to make side bets with each other as to who will last longer in the tournament. As a general principle, these bets should not be made unless they are very small or very large.

The reason being is that you don't really want to have a moderate bet affect your tournament strategy. A hand can come up where the right play for the tournament is the wrong play for your side bet. The examples are so obvious I won't bother going into them.

Of course, if the guy who wants to make the last longer bet with you is a complete idiot, go ahead and make it, and play your normal tournament strategy. After all, that strategy, if you follow the precepts in this book, will tend to make you last longer than most.

However, it has been my experience that the only people who make these bets are those who play a conservative tournament strategy themselves. The only time you might want to bet against them is if they are willing to make a very large bet. In that case, it is worth giving up some tournament equity in order to increase the chances of winning the side bet. If you think they will not be changing their own strategy, you may have a pretty big edge on your side bet if you play super tight.

That of course will hurt your tournament chances. But if you are strictly in it for the money, the bet may be worth making. I never make such bets, and I love it when others at my table do, since it is pretty easy to take advantage of someone who you know is worried about a big last longer bet.

Of course, some people like to make small last longer bets just to keep things interesting. They have no intention of changing their strategy, but just want a little extra action. If you find such things fun, go right ahead.

Freezeout Calculations

It is a common conception that your chances of winning a tournament against equally skilled players are equivalent to the fraction of the total tournament chips that you hold (in your stack). Thus, if you own 15 percent of the chips, your chances of winning are 15 percent. This happens to be right, even though most people don't know why. Assuming everybody is equally skilled and is playing similar strategies, the chance of each player coming in first is precisely in proportion to the size of their stacks.

For the sake of completeness, I would like to demonstrate this fact in the case of two hypothetical players. There is both a mathematical and a logical argument. Let's first do a couple of situations mathematically. (Those who hate this stuff can skip it.)

Suppose Player A has exactly three times as much as Player B. Here is a non-rigorous, but compelling, demonstration that Player A will win this freezeout three quarters of the time. First, what are the chances that Player B will double up? This is basically the same as asking for the chances that Player B will win a freezeout against someone who has the same number of chips as him. Well clearly a freezeout between two equal stacks and two equal players is a fifty-fifty proposition. But in order for Player B to win the freezeout against Player A he must double up (one-half probability) and then double up again (one-half probability). So his chances are one-half times one-half or one quarter.

$$\frac{1}{4} = \left(\frac{1}{2}\right)\left(\frac{1}{2}\right)$$

It is 3-to-1 against him or exactly the ratio of the chips.

Here's a slightly more complicated example. Suppose Player A has twice as many chips as Player B. Let us call Player A's chances of winning the freezeout X. Player B's chances are therefore (1-X). For Player B to win he must first double up, which will give him twice as many chips as Player A, after which he must win a second freezeout where it is he who has twice the chips. So his chances (1-X) require a parlay, the first part of which has a probability of one-half and the second part which has a probability of X (because he is now in exactly the same situation as A originally was). Thus 1-X equals one-half times X.

$$1 - X = \left(\frac{1}{2}\right)X$$

Therefore X equals two-thirds.

$$1 - X = \left(\frac{1}{2}\right)X$$
$$2 - 2X = X$$
$$2 = 3X$$
$$X = \frac{2}{3}$$

Again notice that this corresponds to the ratio of the chips.

There is, however, a more elegant, purely logical proof that equal players in a symmetrical situation must win exactly in proportion to the size of their stacks. Suppose these two players agreed to play the same freezeout everyday for ten years. Given they are equal players, their long run results would necessarily be to break even. Well in order for them to break even, the smaller stack must win exactly the same fraction of times as the fraction of the total chips he possesses. This reasoning extends to any number of players as long as they play equally well, and there is no positional advantage for one compared to the other.

Unfortunately, there is no equally simple technique to calculate the chances of coming in second, third, etc. based solely on the chip count. There are, however, some good ways of estimating these probabilities. (See *Gambling Theory and Other Topics* by Mason Malmuth for further discussion.)

Making Deals

If you are lucky enough to get down to the last two players, you may want to make a deal with your opponent. At this point you are probably playing such high stakes that two or three pots will decide the winner. Meanwhile, the money involved is going to be much more than you are used to playing for. As long as your opponent is also inclined to make a deal, you can probably agree without giving up anything. In other words, he will probably be willing to give you a fair deal, or maybe even one that is mathematically advantageous to you.

With only two players left calculating what you have coming if you ended the tournament immediately is pretty simple. However, the calculation does assume that both players are equal. If you feel like you are clearly the superior player, you might want to get more than the value that these calculations would show.

Keep in mind, however, that your playing superiority probably counts for very little, due to the size of the stakes, unless your edge comes from the fact that he folds too much. If that is the case, you can rob him a little at a time, even at these high stakes, and may in fact have a much greater chance than the chip ratios would indicate, especially if you have enough chips to withstand losing a pot.

You also might shoot for more if you know your opponent is hard up for money, or if you know that he does not know how to calculate the fair price himself. That is up to you.

In the preceeding chapter we showed that with equal players the probability that one player wins is exactly in proportion to his chips. Thus, in a heads-up contest, the player with 60 percent of the chips has a 60 percent chance of winning. With this in mind, it is easy to figure out how much two players should settle for if they want to make a deal and stop the tournament (or perhaps continue playing, but only for the "title").

There are two ways to do this. Suppose first prize is $20,000 and second prize is $12,000. Again we will say that one player has 60 percent of the chips, while the other has 40 percent. The straightforward way to calculate what each player is entitled to is to compute their expected value. The way you do that is you multiply each of the prizes times the chances of winning it. And then you add up those numbers. In this case the leader has a 60 percent chance of winning $20,000, which multiplies to $12,000

$$\$12,000 = (.60)(\$20,000)$$

and a 40 percent chance of winning $12,000, which multiplies to $4,800

$$\$4,800 = (.40)(\$12,000)$$

Add them up. That's $16,800.

$$\$16,800 = \$12,000 + \$4,800$$

The other player has a 40 percent chance for $20,000, which is $8,000, and a 60 percent chance of $12,000, which is $7,200. That adds up to $15,200. Notice that the two figures add up to the proper amount, namely $32,000.

$$\$32,000 = \$16,800 + \$15,200$$

The above method is perfectly fine, and when there are more than two players involved, it is the one you should use. But with only two players, there is an even simpler one.

Notice that at this point the two players are fighting for $8,000, since second place prize money is guaranteed to both of them. The chip leader should win that $8,000 60 percent of the time. He is therefore entitled to $4,800 of that $8,000.

$$\$4,800 = (.60)(\$8,000)$$

The other player is entitled to 40 percent of the $8,000, which is $3,200.

$$\$3,200 = (.40)(\$8,000)$$

The leader should therefore get the $12,000 second prize, plus another $4,800, which is $16,800. The other guy should get 40 percent of that $8,000, or $3,200, plus the second prize of $12,000, which is $15,200. This, of course, is the same answer we got before.

In the case of three players, we cannot be so precise. The reason is that there is no ironclad way to calculate the chances of coming in second and third based on your chip position. Your chances of winning are still the same as the ratio of your chips (with equal players). It is also obvious that the player who has the least chips has the greatest chance of coming in third. But the exact probabilities depend on how the hands are being played, and specifically, how often multiway pots are being played.

In spite of this lack of precision, you should have a pretty good idea of what you should settle for, simply using some common sense. Suppose Player A has $12,000 in chips, Player B has $6,000 in chips, and Player C has $2,000 in chips. Now if this was a one winner tournament, where the winner simply got $20,000, the proper settlement would be just exactly how much they had in front of them, namely, $12,000, $6,000, and $2,000. But the prize structure changes that significantly.

Suppose first prize is $8,000, second prize is $5,000, and third prize is $3,000. Let's look at Player C, the guy with the short stack. His chances of winning are simply his proportion of the chips, namely one-tenth or 10.0 percent.

$$10.0 = \left(\frac{1}{10}\right)(100)$$

But what about his chances of coming in second? Although not perfectly accurate, we can estimate how likely it is that he beats out Player B, the second place man. Since Player B has three times as many chips, Player C has about a 1-in-4 chance of doing that. Since we already gave Player C a 10.0 percent chance of winning, this gives him about a 22.5 percent chance of coming in second

$$22.5 = \left(\frac{1}{4}\right)(100 - 10.0)$$

and thus he comes in 3rd the remaining 67.5 percent of the time or so.

$$67.5 = 100 - 10.0 - 22.5$$

It is now simply a matter of multiplying expectations.

$$(.100)(\$8,000) = \$800$$

$$(.225)(\$5,000)) = \$1,125$$

$$(.675)(\$3,000) = \$2,025$$

When you add those numbers up you get $3,950.

$$\$3,950 = \$800 + \$1,125 + \$2,025$$

Does this surprise you? This seems like quite a bit for a guy with only $2,000 in (tournament) chips. Then again, realize that he had $3,000 guaranteed to him.

The truth is, that in most three-way settlements, the third guy tends to shortchange himself. On the other hand, he might have difficulty getting what he deserves, because the other two guys are miscalculating also. The best way to take advantage of this misunderstanding is to wait until you are the chip leader, or close to it in a three- or four-way finish, especially if the shorter stacks are small, but not tiny.[14] They present more of a danger than most people realize. And you are likely to be able to get a settlement that is better for you than it appears.

---

[14] This is exactly the opposite of other author's advice which recommend striving for a deal when you are short stacked but not otherwise. They are wrong.

Some No-Limit Observations

The only tournaments that are offered no-limit style are hold 'em, and sometimes lowball. No-limit low ball will not be discussed here, since it is offered so infrequently. But no-limit hold 'em is a common tournament event. In fact, it can be found more often in tournaments, than as a sidegame. The final event of most major tournament gatherings is usually a high buy-in no-limit hold 'em event. The "World Poker Champion" is the winner of the final event at the World Series of Poker, the $10,000 No-Limit Hold 'em World Championship.

As a general rule, no-limit hold 'em tournaments are the most profitable for the best players. In a 200 player event, excellent players may have as great as a 1-in-50 chance of winning, and an expected profit as high as four times their buy-in. Such a situation cannot occur in any limit tournament. One reason for the no-limit expert's tournament edge is simply that no-limit is not played very much outside of tournaments, so the top players are facing many neophytes, who are just taking a shot. And, as a general rule, an inexperienced no-limit player will tend to get destroyed by an experienced one.

In other words, a major reason why no-limit tournaments are so profitable to the experts is that they get a chance to play against so many significantly inferior players. This does not occur in limit events, where even the typical player plays pretty well.

There are other reasons besides expertise in no-limit which makes these tournaments great for the "cream of the crop." What I'm referring to is expertise in no-limit tournament strategy. And I am not only talking about the Gap Concept. It is still important, but only as it applies to larger opening bets. In that case, you again need a much bigger hand to call with than you would need to open with. However, if the opening bet is small, that might not be true. If you are one of the better players, you can play a lot of hands when its cheap to come in because of the edges you can obtain from future bets.

Another aspect of tournament strategy that applies especially to no-limit are the adjustments you make depending on the size of your own and your opponents' stack. For instance, it is much more important to avoid marginal confrontations against good players with larger stacks in no-limit than it is in limit. It is also easier to take advantage of small stacks that are trying to survive since they know you can bust them in one hand.[15] Finally, your knowledge of all-in prices is rewarded more in no-limit than in a limit game since all-in situations and decisions as to whether to call all-in or raise someone else all-in, come up much more often.

Don't Turn Good Hands Into Seven-Deuce

Elsewhere in this book I describe a couple of seemingly strange plays that I say are worth making. One involves a big raise before the flop with a lousy hand. The other involves checking top pair and the nut flush draw on fourth street in last position.[16] In both spots I give a brief explanation of an important no-limit concept. But I want to repeat it here as well.

General poker theory teaches that someone who makes a bet or raise into us, hurts us the most when we have a close decision as far as whether or not to call. Certainly when someone bets or raises in a spot where we know that we probably have a better hand than they do, we welcome that action. Almost as obvious is the fact that when their bet or raise indicates we have no chance

---

[15] See Question 48 of the "Hand Quizzes" on page 194 for an example.

[16] See Question 27 of the "Hand Quizzes" on page 169 for an example.

of having the best hand or even of drawing out, that bet or raise does not hurt, since we fold. It may even help, since we avoid committing further chips down the road.

What is less obvious is that, when someone forces us to call when we are probably beaten, or forces us to fold when we still had a decent chance of winning, it is quite bad. And it's especially bad in no-limit, where a person can bet or raise specifically the amount that puts maximum pressure on us. The upshot of all of this is that it is often advisable to refrain from giving your opponent the opportunity to apply this pressure when we have a hand that has decent chances of winning.

What this means is that with such hands we should usually avoid raising or check raising, since that will open up the possibility of getting reraised. It also means strongly considering checking in last position, hands that will hate getting check raised. Again, when I say "hate," I mean being put in a position where your hand may still win, but not often enough where you will welcome that reraise, yet not rarely enough where you can happily fold against it. Notice that this concept may not apply to those times you are in first position since you don't end the betting round if you check.

The reason for this section's title is that beginning no-limit players make a common mistake, putting in fairly big bets or raises before the flop with hands that are very good, but not so good as to welcome a reraise. The problem is that these big bets will almost never be flat called.

Usually they will steal the pot. Maybe even often enough to show a profit. But when they don't, they get reraised big time. So big that you usually have to fold. But that is very sad when your hand is something like

or

These are hands that might have won a big pot had you not played them that way.

Yes, it's true that a raise might win the pot instantly often enough to make it worth doing. If so, go ahead and do it with seven-deuce, not ace-queen suited. Either way you will have to fold if reraised. But if you do it with ace-queen, you have in fact, made it no better than seven-deuce. And this principle applies to later rounds as well.

Ace-King in No-Limit

The specific hand, ace-king, in the specific game, no-limit hold 'em, deserves some special attention.

In limit hold 'em, ace-king is a very good, but not great hand. Especially when it is not suited. But what about no-limit hold 'em? Does its value go up or down when compared to the limit game?

The answer is actually both. When you have lots of money in front of you, ace-king can be a very tricky hand to play in no-limit, because, when you get involved, you usually have made only one pair. Of course that pair is top pair with the best kicker, which, in a limit game, is all you ever need to eventually win all the money. But in no-limit, that same hand can get you into trouble. Weaker players will tend to win a little with it frequently, but sometimes lose a lot with it. And those losses might add up to more than the wins.

But there is another aspect to ace-king in no-limit. That is, if you get all-in with it before the flop, you are almost never in bad shape. The math is simple. Against a pocket pair below kings, your chances are just a tad less than even money. Against two undercards, you are well over 60 percent. Against an ace or king and an undercard you're 75 percent. The only real disaster is if you are against two aces. Now you are less than 10 percent to win. Even against two kings you are about 30 percent.

Put another way, ace-king has at least three reasons to prefer to be all-in before the flop in a no-limit game:

1. It will sometimes be the best hand, even without improving, when all the cards are out. However, many of the times that it would wind up the best hand unpaired, it has been forced to fold by a bettor. Unless, of course, it was all-in.

2. Most of the time that ace-king wins, it is with one pair — a hand that is very tricky to play in no-limit hold 'em, especially to those who are not used to playing that game.

3. A large percentage of the time that ace-king wins a showdown will be when it catches an ace or a king on fourth or fifth street. However, if it is not all-in, it will often not be around to catch those cards, since in no-limit, a bet on the flop is rarely worth calling with merely two overcards.

Thus, we see that moving in before the flop with ace-king is often the best way to play that hand. It is important to understand, however, that it is a lot better to be the bettor when you put all your money in, rather than calling someone else's all-in bet. This is especially true in a tournament where players are apt to throw away some pretty good hands in the face of your all-in bet or raise, including hands that they would have moved in with had they acted before you.

For instance, suppose a typical player might make a big bet, putting you or himself all-in, with a pair of nines or better, as well as ace-king. But if you move in, he will call with only queens or better and maybe ace-king suited. Against a player like this, your results improve quite a bit if you are the aggressor, since you win the pot immediately against three hands (nines, tens, or jacks) that are a favorite over you.

Contrast this with those times you have a pair of pocket jacks against this same opponent. With two jacks, you are better off being the caller because you don't want nines and tens to fold. In general, jacks are a better hand than ace-king offsuit. But usually not when they are used as move in hands.

Let's say once you move in you will only be called by two aces, two kings, or two queens. If you move in with two jacks, your chances are only about 17 percent (when you are called) since that is your approximate chance against each of these three overpairs.

When you have ace-king, you will be about 45 percent against queens, about 30 percent against kings, and about 9 percent against aces. However, since aces and kings are half as likely as queens, given your hole cards, (three combinations each versus six combinations for the queens) your total chances of winning are around 30 percent, which is a lot better than a pair of jacks' chances.

$$0.3 = \frac{(6)(.45) + (3)(.30) + (3)(.09)}{12}$$

The jacks catch up only if there is a possibility they are facing tens or worse. (A definite possibility in many situations, especially late in the tournament.)

Of course, this example is postulating a situation where you have only a 30 percent chance of winning when you move in with ace-king, which might make you wonder how it could be a good play. The answer, of course, is that the play will win the pot without a fight very often, which is the largest aspect to making this a profitable play. Your 30 percent chance of winning when you are called is, however also often needed to make the play an overall positive EV move.

Notice that ace-queen is quite a bit worse off than ace-king if one of the possible calling hands for the opponent is ace-king, as well as the three highest pairs. Not only is ace-queen a big underdog to ace-king, it is also twice as likely to run into a pair of kings. Thus, moving in with ace-queen is not nearly as advantageous as doing it with ace-king.

The best time to move in with ace-king is when moving in is betting two to fives times the size of the pot. When the bet is smaller than this, especially when someone else has already bet, you will almost always get called. That means you do not have the two ways to win that you normally would. That makes your move-in bet equivalent to merely calling. It still might be right to do, but your EV is a lot less since you could be running into small pairs that would have folded to a bigger raise.

Raising or betting more than five times the size of the pot is also a debatable play, not because it won't usually win, but because you might be risking too much to win too little. If raising three times the pot will guarantee your opponent has queens or better when he calls, then raising five times the pot does you little extra good.

Keep this in mind, however. If your stack size is such that you have, say, seven times what's in the pot, there is little point in raising only four times the pot to save money, because anyone who does play with you will almost certainly move you the rest of the way in. Thus, you may as well have moved in yourself. If you do have significantly more than five times the pot, and look down and see ace-king, you may decide that it is better to just call or perhaps raise a small enough amount that you can fold if reraised.

Many of these decisions will depend on how well you play no-limit hold 'em compared to your opponents. Unless you are easily the best player, you might decide to make ace-king an almost automatic move-in hand anytime it has a chance of winning the pot immediately, regardless of the size of the pot. One other advantage to this style is that if you show the hand, it will allow you to do the same thing with a pair of aces, which now might get a call from hands that would have otherwise folded, had they not seen your ace-king move.

Of course, if you do choose to move in with most of your ace-kings, you are choosing to play a style that can get you broke instantly. That goes against some general precepts of tournament play. So don't do it if you know you are the best player, and your chips are many times the size of the pot. And if you do decide that you like being all-in with ace-king before the flop, make sure that's more likely to occur because you are betting as opposed to calling.

When You Are Not the Best Player

In general this book has assumed that you play as well as the best players in the tournament, and better than the rest. But what if you don't? While this possibility will not be addressed in regard to other games, it could be relevant to no-limit. Suppose, for instance, it occurs that you are better than the average player, but definitely not as good as the top players in the tournament.

If this was a pot-limit, rather than a no-limit tournament, the overall situation would be unprofitable. The edge you have against the bad players would not make up for your disadvantage against the best ones. But no-limit is different. Why? Because you can easily get all-in before the flop.

It turns out that a willingness to do this can be a tremendous thorn in the side of a top player. With the exception of two aces, no starting hand can ever feel that comfortable if all the money goes in before the flop. And, if you feel like you are playing against better players, you can take advantage of this fact.

A Proposition

Suppose I walk up to a world champion hold 'em player and offer him the following proposition: A heads-up $5,000 no-limit hold 'em freezeout. We play until one of us has the whole $10,000. The blinds are $100 on the button, and $200 in front of the button. But now I add a little wrinkle. I will move in all of my chips before the flop every hand! It doesn't matter what I have. Clearly, my opponent has an edge. But how big is it?

Suppose I tell him I will play this freezeout if he doubles my win when I win. In other words, he pays me a total of $10,000 those times I win, while I lose only $5,000 when I don't. Should he accept?

Believe it or not, the answer is definitely no. Even if he plays perfectly, he will win this freezeout only about 60 percent of the time. With a little thought you should be able to see why he can't lay 2-to-1.

Let's look at this a little closer. Suppose, for instance, on the first hand he is dealt

What should he do? That hand is a favorite against my two random cards, but the problem is that it is not a 2-to-1 favorite. The actual percentage is 57 percent. Thus, if he calls my bet he is laying 2-to-1 on a 57-to-43 or 1.33-to-1 shot. So it would seem

like he needs to wait until he has a hand that is much more of a favorite than this one. The problem, of course, is that he is being ground down while he is waiting. So when he finally does get a good enough hand to play, (which by the way would be a hand that has a less than 66 percent chance once chips are not even) he not only risks going broke on that hand, he also leaves you with chips, sometimes a significant number of them, even when he wins the confrontation.

The point is that no-limit hold 'em, with all of its skill, is a game where a very aggressive pre-flop strategy can negate that skill. It is like a boxing match where you find yourself against a better fighter. *In* such a case, since you have little chance of winning a 10 or 12 round decision, you are better off going for a knock-out punch, even if that is not your normal style.

The "System"

To show how effective moving in before the flop against good players is, I relate the following true story. A well known casino owner wanted to give his 21 year old daughter the thrill of playing in the final world championship event at the World Series of Poker at Binion's Horseshoe in Las Vegas. He was perfectly ready to put up the $10,000 for her to play in that no-limit event. There was only one problem. She had never played poker in her life.

There was a week to go before the tournament, and he approached me to give her lessons. I appreciated his confidence, but taking someone who has never played poker before and turning them into a champion no-limit player in a week, is an impossible task.

However, I did have an idea. I had been mulling over the concept of doing a lot of moving in before the flop. A few years earlier a very mediocre poker player had won the World Championship making great use of this play. Upon reflection I realized that he had hit upon a strategy which gave him almost as good a chance as the best players. In fact, if those players did not properly adjust to it, he might even have an edge over them. This is especially true because the best players hate to go all-in before the flop, even if they suspect they have a small edge by doing so. They would much rather spar than slug it out. That is, they want to wait for a situation they are almost sure about, rather than speculating that they have the best of it.

Getting back to the casino owner's daughter, I came up with a plan (which the casino owner dubbed "The System") that would take advantage of the above syndrome, and actually give her a chance. Amazingly, this system did not even require that she know how to play poker, or even what beat what. All it required her to do was to move in or fold. (There was a slight problem when she had the big blind. I found a way to deal with that, but we will ignore it to simplify this story.)

The instructions that I gave her, to the best of my recollection, were the following:

1. If someone else has raised in front of you, move in all of your chips with aces, kings, or ace-king suited. Otherwise fold.

2. If no one else has raised in front of you, move in all your chips with any pair, any ace-other suited, ace-king (suited or offsuit), or two suited connected cards, except for four-trey or trey-deuce.

That was basically the whole system. The only other thing besides a separate instruction for the big blind, was that this system was not to be used the first few rounds of the tournament.

The reason The System wasn't to be used at first was that there was too little money in the pot. The $10,000 No-Limit Hold 'em World Championship at the World Series of Poker starts off with blinds of $25 and $50. If she were to move in $10,000, she would be destined to run into a pair of aces well before she had stolen enough antes. Thus, even if all her opponents would throw anything but aces away, The System would be obviously, wrong to use when the blinds were that small. So, for the first two or three levels her instructions were different. They were to throw everything away except aces, and to move in with those aces.

Obviously The System (of selective moving in before the flop) could have been fine tuned further. For instance, I could have adjusted for her position, or whether somebody had already limped in front of her.[17] But I was dealing with someone *who had never played poker* and didn't want to make things more complicated. In spite of this, we actually felt like The System, as it stood, still gave her a chance.

---

[17] See the next chapter "Improving The "System.""

Notice that the hands that she was to move in with (again, when no one raised in front of her) comprised about 13 percent of all the two card combinations. (If you don't know how I got that, stop reading this book right now. You are not ready for it. You don't know enough about poker. And, you deserve to lose.) That means that if she got away with her raises, even if she only stole the ante, her stack would gradually go up, since she was raising often enough to recapture her blinds plus a little more.[18] And of course, there was no reason why she could not get called and still win. In general, if she did get called, she would probably be an underdog, but rarely a big underdog.

I was also counting on the fact that other players were worried about going broke and also worried about players yet to act behind them. I had little doubt that, if she raised in an early position, players on her immediate left would fold hands as good as

or maybe even

---

[18] Of course this assumes a full table. If she got lucky enough to get down to a few players she wouldn't be playing enough hands. That flaw is remedied in the improved system that follows in the next chapter.

or

and, this in fact did happen.

The big problem of course, is that she would eventually run into aces. There were only two ways to withstand that. One, was to beat those aces — most of the hands she would be raising with were about 20 percent against them. The other possibility would be that the player with aces had less money than she did, so she would still have chips to build back up. Because her ante stealing and possible pot winning would mean that her stack was increasing, it was quite reasonable that she would still be alive when she finally did lose to two aces.

Thus, The System, even though it is quite simplistic, actually seemed like it would give her a chance. The math seemed to work out, and there wasn't much that expert players could do to counter it. (As an aside, notice that if I was right, you could argue that it is a *knock* on no-limit tournaments that such a simple system could negate all the weapons of the best players.)[19]

---

[19] Unfortunately, I believe this is true, which is why I have been an advocate of changing the World Championship event to a multi-game format.

So how did she end up? Before I tell you, I must tell you about the tournament that occurred the day before the big one. That was also a no-limit event. It had a much smaller buy-in, perhaps $2,000. Because it was a one day event, the blinds started off proportionately much higher. An ante was also added after the first couple of levels. The casino owner, skeptical of my system, decided to test it himself in this smaller tournament. To make a long story short, The System brought his chips from $2,000 to $35,000! He made the final table, and came in about fifth place. But even that does not properly describe the result, because for some reason, with $35,000 in chips, he decided, for the first time in the tournament, to deviate from The System. Specifically, what he did was call a raise in front of him with

The flop came

and the raiser had two tens. Furthermore, the raiser was the only player who had more chips than he did. Thus there is every reason to believe that had he followed The System, he would have come in at least the top three.

The daughter was not so lucky. After anteing off about $2,000 in the first few levels, The System kicked in and she began increasing her chips. Players were throwing jacks and queens away in the face of her all-in raise, just as expected. She was called one time by ace-king, and won with her pair. But alas, right near the end of the first day, she ran into a big stack with the dreaded aces. I always wonder what would have happened had she won that hand.

Except for confiding in a few friends, I have never told or written about this system before. I am extremely curious as to how strong it really might be. And if it is strong, how much stronger yet a more complex, move all-in, system would be? Most good players would feel very silly playing such a system, so anyone who tested it would more likely be a gambler who does not have his ego involved. Now that I have divulged it, I expect a few of you might give it a try.

One thing is for sure, if you do get into a big tournament and use it, it won't matter much that others know your strategy. There is no good counter strategy which avoids significant risk. In fact, if you use it at a table with some famous world champions, I guarantee you will have them tearing their hair out.

Since the first edition of this book, I have dabbled with a system that takes into account the important factors that the original system ignores: Stack size, blind size, number of limpers, number of players yet to act.

I wrote an article describing a (far from perfect) way to incorporate this information into a bit more complicated move in system. Here is a reprint of that article.

Improving The "System"

In my book *Tournament Poker for Advanced Players,* I recount an experience I had regarding the World Series of Poker $10,000 Championship Event. A wealthy casino owner wanted to give his daughter a thrill by staking her in the tournament. Unfortunately, she had never played a hand of poker of any type.

I was given the assignment to prepare her in only a few hours. It seemed like an impossible task. But I got a flash of inspiration. I realized that no limit hold 'em allowed for a super simple strategy that wasn't all that bad. Namely, either folding or moving in before the flop. Considering the tremendous pressure this would put on other players, especially in a tournament, I might just be able to devise a method that would at least give her a chance.

My book describes the System in more detail, but essentially I had her moving in with any pair, any suited connector, and with ace-king. Everything else she folded. The day before the big tournament the casino owner came in fifth place in a smaller no limit event by following the same System. Unfortunately, in his daughter's case, she ran into pocket aces late on the first day's play and was eliminated, after holding her own for six hours.

The reason why the simple System has a chance, is twofold.

1. Most opponents will not jeopardize their whole stack in close situations (e.g. with two jacks or ace-queen), thereby allowing the System player to steal a lot of small pots.

2. I chose hands that had a decent chance to win when they were called.

But the simple System had at least two obvious problems. They are:

1. It did not take into account stack size versus blind size.

2. It did not take into account how many players were yet to act.

If the rest of the table merely waited for aces, that would probably be good enough to thwart the System at the beginning of the tournament, where moving in was risking so much to win so little. Conversely, if the System player was lucky enough to reach the final five, he or she would be folding so many hands that the blinds would eat them up even if they were never called.

There was no way I had time to teach that girl anything other than the simplest System, drawbacks and all. However, I realized that I could easily improve the System to avoid a lot of these drawbacks. I wasn't willing to do the advanced analysis to make a move or fold system anywhere near perfect. (I invite others to improve the system further). But I realized that some reasonable rules of hand selection that take stack size and position into account would go a long way to making System players much harder to contend with.

Before explaining the improved System, I must point out that there is one situation it doesn't cover. I speak of the times you are in the big blind and nobody raises. You might also include the times you are in the small blind and decide to flick in a chip to call. What you do in these situations is up to you. If you think you play well, then go ahead and play it normally. (But if you lose a lot of chips on those hands you will always wonder what would have happened if you didn't.) If you choose to go to the other extreme you could move in if the flop makes you the nuts (or perhaps the nuts or top set) and check fold if you didn't. An in-between strategy would be to play cautiously, not risking a lot of chips, saving your stack for the System.

Like the original, the improved System also has you either moving in or folding with every starting hand. But unlike the original System, the hands you move in with will depend on various factors. I have combined those factors into one *key number*. After you calculate that key number you will know which hands to move in with.

Here's how you get that key number. First, divide the total amount of the blinds into the amount of your stack. If the blinds were $100 and $200, and your stack was $6,000, that would give you a result of 20.

$$20 = \frac{6,000}{100 + 200}$$

An important result because it is the odds you are laying to pick up the blinds. 6,000-to-300 is 20-to-1. *Important exception:* If no one still in the hand has as many chips as you, use the biggest stack among them. That should be obvious, since your risk is no longer your whole stack.

After you have done this division problem, multiply your result by the number of players, including the blinds, yet to act. So if you were one to the right of the button in the previous example, you would multiply by three and get a key number of 60.

$$60 = (3)(20)$$

When there have been no players coming in in front of you, you are done with the calculation. (When someone has already raised in front of you, reraise all in with aces, kings, or ace-king suited. Otherwise fold.) If there are limpers in front of you, multiply the key number by the number of limpers, plus one. In our example, if there were two limpers the key number would now be 180.

$$180 = (3)(60)$$

Here's how to use the key number to decide whether to move in:

- If the key number is 400 or more, move in only with two aces.

- If the key number is between 200 and 400, move in with AA or KK

- If the key number is between 150 and 200, move in with AA, KK, QQ, or AK

- If the key number is between 100 and 150, move in with AA, KK, QQ, JJ, TT, AK, AQ, or KQ

- If the key number is between 80 and 100, move in with any pair, AK, AQ, KQ, any ace suited, and any no gap suited connector down to 54

- If the key number is between 60 and 80, move in with any pair, any ace, KQ, any king suited, and any suited connector with no gap or one gap

- If the key number is between 40 and 60, move in with all of the above, plus any king

- If the key number is between 20 and 40, move in with all of the above, plus any two suited cards

- If the key number is below 20, raise with any two cards.

Let me reiterate that the above guidelines are very far from perfect. A deep analysis, perhaps with the aid of a computer, would result in more precise and accurate criteria. But what I have suggested here ought to do surprisingly well. The biggest problem I can see would occur if you have frequent raisers on your right. In that case you would need to reraise all in with more than the three hands I recommended.

Let's try a couple of sample hands.

The blinds are $300 and $500. Your stack is $17,000. A player with $12,000 limps in. You are two to the right of the button. The four players yet to act have about ten grand each. You have two sixes. Move in?

Let's calculate the key number. First, notice that the stack size to use is not yours, but rather the largest of the others, $12,000 in this case. Dividing $800 into that number gives us 15.

$$15 = \frac{12,000}{800}$$

Multiply by four players yet to act gives us 60.

$$60 = (4)(15)$$

Multiplying that by two (due to the one limper) yields 120.

$$120 = (2)(60)$$

That's too high to raise with two sixes since the key number needs to be 100 or less. Notice, however, that if there was one less player behind you, you should raise. Or if your stack was below $10,000. (10,000 divided by 8 = 12.5 x 4 x 2 = 100).

Second example. Nine handed. Blinds $100 and $200. First, three fold. You've got $10,000 and some behind you have more. Do you move in with ace-king?

This is simple. Divide 300 into 10,000 to get 33.3. Multiply by the five players yet to act to get a key number of 166.7. Check the key number table. Put the chips in. (But you wouldn't under the gun.)

Again, there is no question that this new System could be improved upon. I'd love to see someone do it. But even without those further improvements, I guarantee that it will give tournament pros fits. If you use it, I will be pulling for you.

Folding Aces

I have often heard or read debates about whether or not it can ever be correct to fold two aces before the flop. Some people adamantly say that that play could never be right,[20] and if you are capable of making it, you should never have entered the tournament in the first place. Others claim that situations where such a fold is correct can come up a lot.

This whole debate is rather silly since the chance that you will ever be in a situation where you are dealt two aces and will considering folding is so small. However, just to put this debate to rest, the fact is there are situations where to do anything but fold them would be wrong.

I have great sympathy for those who play in tournaments mainly to win them, without regard to conserving their chances to win a high place below first. However, taking that attitude to an extreme is a bit ridiculous. For instance, suppose you're at the last table at the $10,000 No-Limit Hold 'em World Championship at the World Series of Poker; the blinds are $10,000 and $20,000, and you have $30,000 in tournament chips. The leader has $2 million, and three other players have exactly $1 million. You are in a distant fifth place.

The prize money distribution is:

- First — $1.5 million
- Second — $1 million
- Third — $700,000
- Fourth — $500,000
- Fifth — $300,000

---

[20] Except in the ultra obvious Super Satellite situation described earlier.

At this point an amazing thing happens. One of the players with $1 million moves in and gets called by the other two $1 million stacks. Barring an unlikely tie, you have just made almost $400,000! You were almost certainly going to come in fifth and get $300,000. And now, barring a tie in this three-way pot, you will have $700,000 sewn up. What a lucky break! Except for one thing. You look down at your hand and see

Now what?

The rules of this tournament say that if you go broke at the same time as someone else your prize money depends on how much you started with at the beginning of the hand. So if you play those two aces and lose, you are paid for fifth place only.

If you played the aces and won, you would, again, barring ties, find yourself in a three-way situation having $120,000 in chips against a $2 million dollar stack and a $2,910,000 stack. If you stayed out of the hand you would have $30,000 facing a $1million and a $3 million stack. Surely I need not bore you with the math that proves that the extra measly $90,000 and the few extra percent chance it gives you of walking away with first or second prize is not worth the significant risk of blowing $400,000 when your aces do not stand up against the three other players. That will happen almost half the time.

So to play aces here means you have thrown away $400,000 maybe 40 percent of the time, while the other 60 percent of the time you have given yourself, at best, another 10 percent chance to move to second and gain $300,000, and a few percent extra chance to go into first and gain $800,000. About the only person who should consider playing two aces in this spot is me, since the extra book sales a World Championship would give me might swing the decision to a call.

Why the
First Day Leader
at the WSOP Never Wins

The $10,000 No-Limit Hold 'em World Championship at the World Series of Poker, which is the final event, lasts five days. (It used to be four.) The game is no-limit hold 'em. After the first day the chip leader typically has about $65,000. I cannot remember a time, although it has probably happened once or twice, where that chip leader has pulled down a major prize. Considering that starting with $65,000 should give you more than a 10 percent chance to get to the last table, especially in the days when there were less than 300 entrants, it seems odd that these first day leaders don't get there. This might seem doubly true because the chip leader not only has the most chips, but presumably is also playing quite well to accumulate those chips.

But this syndrome is not really odd at all. Remember that the first day of the WSOP involves very small blinds culminating late in the day with $100 and $200 blinds and a $50 ante. If you are following the precepts in this book, your first priority is not to go broke. So you would not, for example, risk a large amount of chips on iffy situations. Playing this way normally results in moving your chips up to a maximum of $25,000 or so by the end of the first day.

Often, good players playing this way end up with less than $15,000. There is, of course, always a chance that a perfect hand will come up that will allow you to win more. But generally, the only way to highly increase your stack is to play in a style that we know is not correct.

Now, let's say the tournament started with 400 players, 200 of whom are using correct tournament precepts, and 200 of whom are taking too many chances (and also may be simply playing badly). At the end of the first day there should be about 230 players left. About 160 of them will come from the tighter group. They will have an average of, let's say $19,000 each. That's $3,040,000.

$$\$3,040,000 = (160)(\$19,000)$$

Only about 70 of the gambling group will be left. They will have an average of about $13,700.

$$\$13,714 = \frac{\$4,000,000 - \$3,040,000}{70}$$

However, their variability is a lot higher. In the first group, most of the players will have between $10,000 and $25,000. In the second group, many will have less than they started with, but a few will have much more.

Usually the chip leader will come from this second group. But this second group is comprised of players who are playing incorrectly. Notice that the 200 original good players who started with $2,000,000 as a whole, have increased their stake to $3,040,000. The other group, as a whole, went from $2,000,000 to $960,000.

$$\$960,000 = \$4,000,000 - \$3,040,000$$

(I use these numbers merely to illustrate a point. In real life the discrepancy is probably not this clear cut.) Nevertheless because of the volatility of the play of the second group, it is still quite likely that the chip leader will emerge from this group. That being the case, it is not surprising that the chip leader eventually goes down the tubes during the remaining days of the tournament.

Don't get me wrong. Even during the first day of the final tournament of the WSOP you should play selectively aggressively, and certainly not timidly. You merely avoid large pots that are close decisions to ensure survival. It is just that the blinds are too small to allow you to more than double or triple up that first day if you are playing right, unless the cards are completely running over you.

Other Topics
Afterthought

While no-limit hold 'em is a great game that certainly can be a terrific test of courage and skill, it does have an "Achilles heel" in a tournament format. Weak players who frequently move in before the flop can negate much of the skill of their better playing opponents and dramatically improve their chances of success.

A few years ago, a totally unknown player finished second in the $10,000 No-Limit Hold 'em World Championship at the World Series of Poker by playing in precisely this fashion. He literally terrorized the field, and several of the well known top players felt that his play was absolutely brilliant. In fact, we know that in a sense this really was the case because he had hit upon a simple strategy that made him a very formidable opponent.

The point of this is that our world champion should probably not be determined by a no-limit tournament. Perhaps a tournament consisting of a combination of limit games would be better. But I suspect that tradition will prevail and large buy-in no-limit contests will always be the final event at the major tournaments.

Part Four

Hand Quizzes

Hand Quizzes
Introduction

We now come to what for many of you will be the most important part of the book. This is the section which will put the concepts we have learned into action.

. When playing poker, it is very important to be able to make your decisions quickly. But they also need to be made accurately. Knowing and understanding theory isn't the same as sitting at the poker table and playing a few hands. Under pressure it is easy to forget and/or confuse concepts and make mistakes. So what can we do to keep this from happening?

Well, one thing is to work through some tournament hands that illustrate many of the ideas we have been talking about. And that's exactly what follows.

Quiz

1. You are midway through an ace-to-five lowball tournament and have average chips. Everyone folds to you, and you raise with

one to the right of the button. Only the big blind, also with average chips, calls you. He draws two cards. How many should you draw?

Answer: Many of you are probably wondering why the heck this is the first question? We have never even discussed how to play lowball tournaments (because they are so rare) and certainly not discussed how many cards to draw. Plus most of you are probably unfamiliar with this game. But this is a wonderful question to illustrate tournament principles and how they might differ from a sidegame.

Remember the idea is to maximize your chances of winning pots and to avoid losing bets whenever the alternative (namely gambling) has little or no extra EV. Because of that, the right play in this tournament situation is almost certainly to *stand pat.* That play, though debatable in a sidegame, is pretty clearcut in a tournament.

In a sidegame, you would probably draw one (rather than two by the way) to help you win more money after the draw much of the time. If you draw, it is fairly likely you'll make a hand that you can bet and get paid off (by something like a ten or a jack low). But this gamble is not worth it in a tournament.

Keep in mind that the rules of lowball practically force the first player to bet if he makes a seven low or better. Since you stood pat, it is likely that if he comes out betting into you he will have such a hand. Thus, one advantage of standing pat is that you lose less money, compared to drawing, those times he makes a seven. Because if he bets, you fold.

The other advantage is that when he makes a mediocre hand, typically nine through queen, you will always win, since he will not suspect a bluff from your pat hand, but would have, had you drawn. This is especially true in a tournament.

What you give up by standing pat are the calls you would get after the draw when you make a somewhat better hand than he does. Depending on how he plays, that extra call could make drawing slightly better mathematically. But the extra risk you take for that slight gain in EV is probably not worth it in a tournament. So unless you think your opponent has read this book, stand pat.

2. Somewhere in the middle of a limit hold 'em tournament. No one at your table is on a short stack. Players are playing typically tight. You are under the gun with

What do you do?

Answer: The Gap Concept means that in situations like this you almost always fold or raise. It also implies that you should raise with more hands than you would in a sidegame, including some you would usually fold, because of the much greater chance of stealing the blinds. In spite of all that, those of you who thought you should raise with J♣T♥ are probably wrong. That hand is simply too weak in first position at a full table. The only exception is if you see your opponents are playing ridiculously tight, in which case raising with this hand might be okay.

3. You are at the last table of a seven-card stud tournament. There are five players left. You have slightly less than average chips. You raise with

Another player goes all-in with a nine showing, and a third player, with more chips than you, calls with a ten showing. The nine catches an ace, the ten catches an offsuit four, and you catch a queen. There is no side pot at this point. The ace is all-in, the ten checks; what should you do?

> **Answer:** The idea that you should "check it down" when you are in a three-way pot, where one person is all-in, is usually wrong. If you have a clearly superior hand, you should normally bet, even though that gives the all-in hand a better chance to survive (when others fold). There is however, a situation where you would make this play in a tournament, even though you would not in a regular game. In order for this technique of checking down to be correct, you usually need four things to be the case:

1. You are already in the money or very close to it.

2. You are not a significant favorite over the other player with chips.

3. You are fairly low in chips, and thus are strongly rooting for someone else to go broke.

4. There is a pretty good chance that if you let the third guy in, by checking, he will end up beating the all-in player while you do not.

If all these criteria are met, you should, in fact, check on that round. (Although you should not continue to check if succeeding cards turn you into a bigger favorite.) In this particular question all those criteria are in fact met. So, in this precise case, the answer is probably to check.

4. There are two people left; you have $12,000 in chips and your opponent has $10,000. It is no-limit hold 'em. You are up against a world champion. You call a $500 raise before the flop with

The flop is

You are first to act. What do you do?

Answer: Move all-in. If your opponent is aggressive, I will also accept the answer to check raise all-in. What I won't accept is checking and calling, or making a small bet.

Moving all-in with this hand is a fairly routine play if you are betting somewhere around the size of the pot. Betting nine times the size of the pot, as I recommend, is not generally good poker, no matter what your hand. But in this particular case, where you are not likely to outplay this guy, you are better off attempting to let the outcome ride on one hand.

In this example, you are about even money against most one pair hands, and only a slight dog to most better hands. As long as your opponent plays better than you do, getting all the money in on the flop is almost certainly the correct play.

5. It is the middle of an Omaha high-low-split eight-or-better tournament, and no one is on a short stack. Players are playing as they typically do. The under the gun player raises, and you are next. You hold

What should you do?

Answer: In a normal game the correct decision is close between calling and folding. In a tournament, reraising is another possibility, since it gives you a better than normal chance of being heads-up against the raiser, while having position on him. If you change the ten to a king, I would strongly consider that play since an ace on board is apt to pair both of you. But given the cards I specified, the correct play in a tournament is almost definitely to fold.

6. It is the second level of seven-card stud and no one is on a short stack. Players are playing typically. A deuce brings it in; a jack and a deuce fold; you are next with

Behind you is a queen, two kings, and a seven, in that order. What should you do?

Answer: This is a good example of a play that probably changes because you are in a tournament. In a sidegame, you have a close decision, but should probably lean toward folding. In a tournament, you should probably raise. Your chances of stealing the ante are too great. Also your chance of getting reraised by someone without a big pair are reduced.

7. It is late in a limit hold 'em tournament, but still not that near the money tables. You are in the big blind with

everyone folds to the button, who raises, and you have just enough to call that raise. The small blind folds. Do you call?

Answer: You are getting 3½-to-1 odds. Even if he has two over cards or a pair below jacks, 3½-to-1 is much more than enough odds to make the call right. Only if he has a pair of jacks or better would the call be wrong. There is no reason to believe his hand has to be anywhere near that good. Furthermore, survival to pick up a prize should not yet enter your thinking. So your decision should be based purely on your pot odds. (As they would if you were somehow in this situation in a sidegame.) You have a clear call.

8. There are four tables left. You have an average amount of chips in a limit hold 'em tournament. The last two tables are in the money. Your opponents are playing well. Three of them limp in before the flop. You are on the button with

Should you raise?

Answer: This is a clear raise in a non-tournament game. The question is whether the tournament situation turns this hand into merely a call. Although I think it is close, and I would say otherwise if it was earlier in the tournament, I believe it does. The reason I would not raise is threefold:

1. It is more likely than normal that your hand is not so great in comparison to the other players. They are playing quite tightly, trying to avoid elimination, and some might choose to limp in with hands that dominate or tie the A♥J♥.

2. The extra EV you gain by raising is partially counterbalanced by the fact that making the pot bigger will force you to often lose more money because you have to take one or two extra cards off. For instance, if the flop is

(Giving you two over cards and a three flush) you would often have to at least call a flop bet.

    Of course you would win some of those pots, but still, in a tournament small chances of winning big pots, which means large chances of losing some bets is not a good situation, even when the EV is slightly positive. Not raising avoids putting yourself into this situation.

3. Not raising will increase your chances of winning the pot. This, even though not raising will sometimes result in one of the blinds, who would have folded a raise, beating you. In spite of that, just calling increases your chances because your opponents are getting lower odds when you, or someone else, bets into them later on. They

are, therefore, more apt to fold a hand that might have drawn out on you. Also, by not raising, you are more likely to be bet into when an ace or jack flops, which allows you to thin the field.

Of course, the downside of making this play to increase your chances of winning the pot, is that the pots you win will be smaller. However, late in the tournament, when your chip stack is not high enough to ensure getting into the money, I believe the upside outweighs the downside, although I think it is close. (It is so close that I am sure that you should raise if your hand was ace-king suited and possibly ace-queen suited.)

9. You are at the last table with seven players left in a seven-card stud tournament. A 2♣ brings it in, and an 8♥ raises. You're next and have

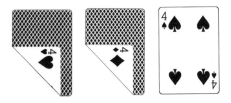

The player on your immediate left does not have enough chips to play a hand to the river. He is showing a T♦. Behind him is a 4♣, Q♠, and J♠. You are in fifth place, chip wise. Do you call or reraise?

Answer: In sidegames, it is reasonable to slowplay small rolled up hands, even when one of your trip cards is out. In a tournament, it is less reasonable because, with close decisions, it is usually better to maximize your chances of winning the pot. This is especially true at the last table.

However, this particular situation is different. You have a chance to bust the short stack, which is particularly good for you since you are on low chips yourself. If you just call, the short stack will almost certainly play a pair of tens and may even play three high cards such as

since the raiser had an eight showing. If you reraise, however, he will certainly fold those hands, not only because of the strength that you showed, but also because of the two overcards behind him. Plus, he would see an opportunity to sit back and root for you to dissipate your chips. So in this specific situation I believe you should deviate from the normally correct tournament strategy of reraising and merely call.

10. It is the last table of a limit hold 'em tournament. The blinds are \$500 and \$1,000. You have \$2,000 left and have to put in the big blind, leaving you with \$1,000. The two players on your left both have \$1,500 in front of them. The other three players have more than \$30,000 each. Everyone folds to the button who raises to \$2,000. The small blind folds. You have

Should you call?

Answer: Even though you know the button will raise with almost anything, which means your K♠T♠ will win more than half the time, this is an extraordinary circumstance. If there is a big money jump between fourth, fifth, and sixth place, you should probably throw your hand away and the next hand as well. There is an excellent chance that this strategy will move you into fifth place and a good chance it will move you all the way into fourth place. That is because the two players on your left must go all-in with anything before you have to put your last $500 in. Notice also, if you did play and win, you are still far below the third place player. Thus you should fold K♠T♠ and similar hands in this situation.

I would not take this to an extreme, however. With two aces, your chances of winning are so great, I believe you should call and take the risk of going broke. That is because winning here brings you up to $4,500 which gives you an even better chance of winning at least fourth place and some small chance of finishing higher.

11. Seven-card stud. Middle of the tournament. No one is on a short stack. A 2♠ brings it in; a 7♥ folds, and you are next with

Behind you in order are the 6♣, 5♣, Q♦, and J♥. Should you call raise or fold?

Answer: This is a perfect example of a situation where the fact that you are in a tournament will probably change your strategy. In a sidegame, this hand is normally not quite worth playing. However, in a tournament, against players who are playing typically, you have a raising hand. That is because small pairs and any three card straights will now probably fold, even though they might have called in a sidegame.

This answer is, of course, a generic one. If for some reason you find that players are playing differently from how typical tournament players play, you will adjust accordingly. But as a general principal, in seven-card stud tournaments, you should raise with all but your worst hands when no one else is yet in, and you have the (unduplicated) highest card showing.

12. There are two tables left in a limit hold 'em tournament with six players at each table. Most of the money goes to the last nine at the final table. The blinds are $200 and $400. You have $3,000, and it is less than average. The two players in the blinds have about $1,200 each. Everyone folds to you on the button, and you have

What should you do?

Answer: Even though you are in jeopardy of not making the last table, not raising in this situation would be wrong if the players in the blinds are typical. There is simply too great a chance that you will steal those blinds.

I say this because of the precise size of their stacks. If they had either more or less, they would call you fairly liberally. (With more, because there is no reason not to play normal poker strategy, and with less, because they can't wait any longer.) But with these size stacks, they will probably elect to throw away marginal hands in the hopes that something better will come along or that they can sneak into the last table with their remaining chips.

You should take advantage of that. Keep in mind that you will still have $2,200 if your raise gets called and you give up. That often will still be enough to make the last table.

I might have answered this question differently if your stack had been significantly smaller. It is also not irrelevant that your hand included a king. You just might hit that king and bust one of the blinds.

13. It is the last table. You are the chip leader in a limit hold 'em tournament. You raise with

and get one call behind you by a player who is now all-in. You also get calls from the two blinds. There is no side pot. The flop comes

Both blinds check. Should you bet?

Answer: If you do not bet, the player who is all-in is in big trouble. More so if you check again on fourth street. That is why it is common practice for players to have sort of a gentleman's agreement to check to each other any hands that are not very strong when there is a player who is all-in. This is doubly true when there is no side pot. By playing this way, everyone increases their chances of moving up one place.

But besides possibly being ethically wrong, that strategy is also strategically wrong when you have a lot of chips. It will almost never matter to you whether the next person who goes broke is the all-in guy or somebody else. It only significantly matters to those who are in danger of going broke next, if the all-in guy doesn't. In this particular situation, betting the flop with ace-king will get the blinds to fold more than they normally would. Not only because they are less apt to gamble with higher prizes coming up, but also (maybe) because they don't think that you would violate this supposed well known principal of checking mediocre hands down when someone is all-in. So go ahead and bet. Sure it might allow the all-in player to win a pot and survive where he might otherwise not. So what? It also might win you a pot with no further risk (since you get your last bet back when the blinds fold).

14. In the middle of a seven-card stud tournament, no one is short stacked at your table, you have called a raise on third street with

and one other spade is out. You have two opponents. On fourth street you catch the K♦ and there is a bet and a call. Should you call?

> **Answer:** This is probably an example of a situation in which you would switch your play between a sidegame and a tournament. It is often marginally correct in a sidegame to take one more card off when you break off a fairly live three flush on fourth street, especially if you catch a big card. However, if you are one of the better players, in a tournament you should usually fold in this same situation.
>
> The problem with this particular hand is that taking a card off is not only risking one bet that will usually be lost, but that it will often risk additional bets that will also be lost. You don't need to get involved in these types of close gambling situations if you are a good tournament player.

15. It is the middle of an Omaha high-low-split eight-or-better tournament. No one is on a short stack. Two players have folded. You have

What do you do?

> **Answer:** Unlike hold 'em, it is often right, playing Omaha high-low-split eight-or-better, to merely limp in, even when no one else has limped in front of you. This is because there are more hands in Omaha that crave multiple opponents behind them, and smaller chances to win the whole pot with a raise before the flop. The above hand is a good example of

one, that in early position, in a ring game is usually best to just call with. However, this would not normally be the case in a tournament. Because of the way players typically tighten up in the face of a raise while playing tournaments, it means that raising with this hand is more likely to instantly win the blinds. While merely limping is not as apt to result in a multiway pot. Thus you should probably raise.

16. Three players have folded; no one is short stacked, and you have

in a limit hold 'em tournament. Call, raise, or fold?

Answer: Notice that I did not mention how far along you are in the tournament because it doesn't matter. If opponents are playing the way they typically do, the Gap Concept applies perfectly here and you must raise.

There are sidegames where calling would be better because you will entice many to limp behind you. There are also sidegames where folding should be considered because a raise will not get out hands like ace-jack, king-ten, or queen-jack. But neither of these types of games is likely to be what you are facing in a tournament.

A limp will not entice other limps, but a raise will get out lots of hands that you want out, and may even steal the blinds. As a general rule, once a few players have folded, you should never limp before the flop in a limit hold 'em tournament, and your raising hands don't have to be that great.

17. There are four tables left in a no-limit hold 'em tournament. Prizes are paid to the last two tables. The blinds are $100 and $200. You have $4,200, which is slightly less than average, and you are holding

in the big blind. All fold to the button, who puts in $800 and has $6,000 left. The small blind folds. What should you do?

Answer: There are three possible reasons not to move all-in. One would be that your opponent is very tight and will thus have the dreaded aces or kings a significant portion of the time. Another reason would be that your opponent plays badly from the flop on allowing you to extract extra money when an ace or a king hits and save money when you don't have the best hand. A third reason would be that you are far superior to most of the players in this tournament and would hate to risk going broke with this non-paired hand.

These three reasons are legitimate, but almost always not good enough. I would still move in here almost every time, and so, probably, should you.

18. It is the middle of a limit hold 'em tournament; no one is on a short stack; five players fold before the flop; the next player (a very good tournament player) raises. You have

What should you do?

Answer: Once this many players fold, it is almost never correct to flat call a raiser unless you are in the big blind. This is even more true in a tournament than in a sidegame. Because players tend to play a little bit tighter, however, your reraising hands need to be a bit better. With one important exception. That is when the original raiser is familiar with the Gap Concept. (Most of the best players were, even before I wrote this book.) When such a player raises with no one else in yet, his hands will, on average, be a little bit worse than they would be in a sidegame. Thus, your reraising hands can be a bit worse too. Not only because of his hand, but because the players behind you will throw all but the very best hands away for three bets cold. Clearly then, you should reraise with your two jacks in this situation. (However, against a less expert-type player, it might be right to fold.)

19. It is a seven-card stud tournament, midway through the levels. There are no short stacks. A 2♥ brings it in. Three players fold, and a good tournament player, showing an A♠ raises. Two more fold, and you have

Your cards are live. What should you do?

Answer: This question is similar to the one preceding it. The player with the A♠ is very likely not to have aces. However, unlike hold 'em, reraising, especially in a tournament, may not be a good idea.

There are two differences between this and the previous hold 'em example. One is that a pair of jacks is less likely to be the best hand in stud, especially when it is facing an open ace. The second reason is that the original raiser has a much better idea of what you have, and can take advantage of it. In the hold 'em example, the first raiser has to be scared that your hand is even better than two jacks. Not nearly as much so in stud. Still, J♦T♦J♣ is far too good a hand to throw away, even in a tournament. That's probably true even if you were sure you were facing two aces. So you must at least call.

Reraising however, while not a terrible play, opens yourself up to his reraising, which in turn will make the pot so big that you will usually have to play the hand all the way to the river. This is not the kind of situation you want to be in when you are one of the best players in the tournament, i.e. playing a big pot as a probable underdog.

Therefore, I believe that the right answer to this question is to merely call unless your opponent will raise with practically any three cards. Unlike most of the other questions, I do believe the answer is close. But I included it in order to illustrate this tournament principle that applies specifically to stud.

20. Back to hold 'em. Again, a mid-level situation, with no short stacks. Four players limp, including the small blind. You check in the big blind with

The flop is

You check. Someone bets and gets two calls. What should you do?

Answer: In a sidegame, I would usually just call here. In a tournament, I would always just call. The plan is to root for a blank, and go for a check raise on fourth street. When your hand holds up and you play it that way, you usually win at least as much as you would have had you check raised the flop. But that is only part of the reason you don't raise the flop. The bigger reason, which takes on more importance in a tournament, is that you can save money when a bad card comes off. The worst card is probably an eight; other bad cards are queen, jack, nine, and seven. When they come off you should check again, and be prepared to fold if it is a cold raise to you. The general principle here is that the often used (by experts) tactic of waiting until fourth street to see if a bad card comes off, is even more indicated in limit hold 'em tournaments.

Note: In this question I did not have you coming right out betting on the flop because I wanted to make a point. Do not infer that I believe checking the flop is necessarily always the right play.

21. Getting back to stud, that same hand where the A♠ raised and you flat called with the J♣ showing and a J♦T♦ in the hole. On fourth street he catches an offsuit 7♥, and you catch a T♥. He bets. You are now almost sure he has aces, given that bet, so you just call. On fifth street you catch a 7♣ which is the same suit as your upcard. He catches a 5♦ and bets again. What should you do?

Answer: In our book, *Seven-Card Stud for Advanced Players,* we address the situation where you have two hidden pair on fifth street and are facing a bet from an obvious big pair (or possibly better hand). We point out that raising here is probably not as good an idea as waiting until the next card, in order to see whether he pairs his board. If he does, you save money. And if he doesn't, you get your raise in on sixth street.

However, the problem with waiting is that you will sometimes catch a card on sixth street that keeps him from betting into you. When there may be many such cards it is usually right to make the fifth street raise. But because this is a close decision, I believe the proper strategy in most tournament situations is to wait. This is yet another example of opting for the less volatile play when the two alternatives are close, and it is similar to the hold 'em example above. As I've been emphasizing throughout this book, if you are one of the best players in the tournament, you should avoid committing excess chips early in a hand on close decisions, not only because you are gambling with those chips, but also because your making the pot bigger may force you to gamble further with even more chips.

22. Seven-card stud, midway through the tournament. The 2♣ brings it in, the J♠ raises. Three other unduplicated cards below a jack call, including a couple of short stacks. You are last with

What do you do?

> **Answer:** I threw this question in to keep anyone from trying to guess my answers merely because I asked the question. That is a natural inclination when you take a quiz, but I don't want you doing that. Just answer these questions as if they came up while you were playing. Don't try to figure out what tricky reason I may have had to ask them. Here you raise of course.

23. You are down to five players in a seven-card stud tournament. Everyone has approximately the same number of chips and cannot go broke on one hand. The 2♣ brings it in, the J♠ raises. You are next with

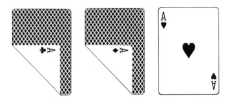

What do you do?

Answer: In a tournament it is important to win the pots you play. It is doubly important when you are at the last table. Slowplaying big hands to suck other people in, is not right nearly as often as it would be in a sidegame. Getting heads-up with the best hand is something you should usually be striving for.

However, all of these principles assume that you are choosing between two fairly close plays. This one is not close. With three rolled up aces you give up way too much when you knock everyone out. Yes, a reraise will increase your chances of winning the pot. But your chances are already so high that you must try to win an even bigger pot here.

Had your three-of-a-kind been smaller than some of the upcards, the right play would probably reverse, and you should reraise, even though you might not in a sidegame. But it would be a sin not to try to get as much as you could out of these three bullets.

24. In the middle of a limit hold 'em tournament you are in the big blind, with

Four players limp. The flop is

Everyone checks. The turn is the 9♥. Everyone checks. The last card is the J♠. What do you do?

> **Answer:** In the text I point out a similar situation where I recommend bluffing on the river after everyone has checked twice. But this is different. Here the cards are getting higher, not lower, and are thus much more likely to have hit someone. You would be getting less than 3-to-1 on your bluff, and I don't believe it is worth trying.

25. It is the first hour of the $10,000 No-Limit Hold 'em World Championship at the World Series of Poker. The blinds are $25 and $50. The first player raises to $300. The second player calls. Two more players call behind him. You make it $2,000 to go with

The initial raiser folds. The first caller folds. The second caller moves in $10,000. You have never seen him before. The other caller folds as well. Should you call?

Answer: I bring up this question because I have seen this type of situation occur no less than three times. In all three cases the kings called. In all three cases those with the kings needed to have their heads examined. Seriously, a call in this spot is insane. I mean, what do they think that guy had? Sure he played the hand oddly. You would have expected him to raise the first time around if he had aces. But that still does not change anything. He has aces. (Or just maybe kings. But even if he will play two kings this way you still can't call since there is only one combination of kings he could have versus six combinations of aces. At this point you would be getting odds of approximately 8-to-5 if you called. Assuming this occurred 70 times, and he had aces 60 times, and kings 10 times, the results would be: Ten times you would split the pot and make about $2,500 compared to folding, eleven times you would make about $13,500 compared to folding, and 49 times you would lose $8,000, plus go broke. So you can see that even if he might have kings, calling is horrible.)

Why am I so sure he has aces or just maybe kings? Put yourself in his shoes. He has to seriously worry that you have a pair of aces. You, after all, put in that big reraise against all those other players. Is he going to jeopardize all of his chips in the hopes you don't? Does it make any sense that he would do this with a pair of queens? You do sometimes see this play with ace-king suited. But not when it costs so much, and not when it is so likely that it is facing aces or kings.

Those three players who made this call with the two kings were all considered good players. But I lost a little respect for each of them. They were not able to adjust to a unique situation. All they knew was that their hand was two kings, a ridiculous hand to fold pre-flop in normal situations, and that the other player's play did not coincide with the way two aces would normally be played. But they did not have the skill to realize that those factors were irrelevant. As a secondary error, they did not understand that even if it was close, they should not be moving all their chips in this early in a tournament since all three were in the top 10 percent of all players skill wise.

I should point out that the reason this fold is so clear cut is that the initial blinds were so small compared to the size of the stacks. That ratio is not true to this degree in just about any other poker tournament. And as the stacks shrink compared to the blinds, it will never be as undebatable to fold two kings before the flop as it is here.

26. It is the beginning of a limit hold 'em tournament. Four people limp in. And you have

on the button. What should you do?

Answer: Raise. This is the right way to play in a sidegame. In a tournament, you would seriously consider flat calling. You don't want to risk an extra bet with a very slight edge, and more importantly, you don't want to increase the size of the pot to the point where you will have to risk even more chips in a situation where you will probably not win the pot. Except, this is the first level. Because of that, tournament preservation strategies don't matter much. You are playing well within your bankroll. So if a play is even slightly right to do, you should do it.

A secondary advantage is that it will create the impression that you are not playing an especially tight tournament strategy, even though you, in fact, will be as soon as the stakes are raised. Thus, the play is especially advantageous when your table will not be broken up for awhile.

27. It is the middle of a no-limit hold 'em tournament. None of the relevant players are short stacked. The blinds are $25 and $50, and you have $5,000 in front of you. Two people limp in. You raise $200 with

The blinds fold and the limpers call. The flop is

Both players check. You bet $600. They both call. The next card is the 2♥. They both check. How much should you bet?

Answer: The answer to this question happens to be the same for both tournaments and sidegames. However, to play it incorrectly is even worse in a tournament. The answer is well known to good no-limit players, but may not be to you if your only no-limit experience is tournaments. Anyway, the amount you bet is $0. Had the fourth card not been a heart, it may or may not have been right to bet this hand, depending on how likely you think you are being trapped. But when the heart comes, it is usually very wrong to bet.

The principle is one that was mentioned in the text. You should not bet in last position, or raise another bettor, if you will hate him raising back. This concept rarely relates to limit poker because there are not many times when you would truly hate someone raising you. The worst that happens is that you lose an extra bet. But in no-limit, a raise can be large enough where you have to throw your hand away, even though your chances of winning are significant. In this particular situation, if you bet, say $1,500, and one of the other two players check raised all-in, you are in major trouble. Almost certainly you are beat.

The problem is that you have a draw to the nuts, but not the pot odds to call. (Actually, even if you did have good enough pot odds you're still in major trouble because you are now forced to call with a hand that will probably lose.) Thus, in situations like this, you should almost always check because you would hate to see a raise.

Without the four hearts, you could bet, because a raise means you are probably drawing dead. So folding does not hurt you. You also can bet if your hand is so good that you welcome the raise. But neither of those situations exist here. Thus you take a free card.[21]

28. The game is limit hold 'em. The stakes are $100-$200 with a $50 and $100 blind. All fold to the button who makes it $200. The small blind folds. You started this hand with $300 and have $200 after putting in the blind. Your hand is

---

[21] Keep in mind that this play assumes you are in last position. If you are not, the right answer is not as clear because you cannot prevent further betting with a check. So you might want to bet yourself. But there is still a good reason to check. It is that this allows you to have high implied odds if you merely call the bet behind you.

Should you call, reraise all-in, or fold?

Answer: Before answering this question, we do have to agree on some assumptions — assumptions that would accurately describe the vast majority of opponents. Number one is that they will raise with a lot of hands. That is a standard play in this spot. Second, we assume that a reraise before the flop by you will always be called. Obviously. He's getting $550-to-$100 odds on that all-in reraise. Third we assume that if you call before the flop, and check on the flop, he will usually bet. I am sure you agree that almost all opponents will play this way. So let's start the analysis.

First, let's see if you should possibly throw the A♣2♦ away. You are getting 3½-to-1 on his raise which would make this an easy call if you were all in. The problem is that extra $100 in your stack. Might that change things?

If you shove it in before the flop, the real odds you are getting are no longer $350-to-$100. They have gone down to $450-to-$200 or 2½-to-1. Is it worth taking those odds with A♣2♦?

Well, of course it is. If he would raise with anything, your hand would actually be a slight favorite. But even if he was throwing bad hands away, there is no way his remaining hands would beat you anywhere near the 69 percent or so needed to make it right to fold.

This means that we have established that folding cannot be right. We have also showed that reraising shows a profit (if the big blind is counted as no longer yours). That beats folding and breaking even.

In fact, I believe most players would reraise in this spot. But there are alternatives. You could merely call before the flop. And then depending on what came, you could bet, check and call, or check and fold. Let's look at these alternatives.

First, notice that, if you always called before the flop, and then check and called on the flop you would essentially be in the same position as you would have been had you raised before the flop. Given the fact that your check will almost always elicit a bet, playing that way results in a showdown for the $650 pot. Just like your reraise would. So this strategy gains nothing over the all-in raise.

But what about checking and sometimes folding? Oh yeah? When would you do that? You would be getting $550-to-$100 on his flop bet and you have an ace. Between the times you catch an ace and the times ace high wins unimproved, your chances would always total more than the necessary 15 percent to win the pot.

So checking and folding is out. And checking and always calling is no better than reraising preflop. What about calling before the flop and betting out on the flop? The problem of course with this play is that it allows your opponent to save a bet when he flops nothing. Moving in before the flop prevents this. But wait. What odds is he getting on your flop bet? Again it is $550-to-$100. Suppose the flop is

and he has

Your bet has probably caused him to fold a hand with six outs! He is less than a 5½-to-1 dog so he costs himself money by folding. Money (actually EV) that you gained. Had you reraised preflop you would have won an extra $100 most of the time to be sure. But that isn't enough to make up for the risk of losing the pot on the turn or the river.

It is true that there are not too many flops that your bet will make him "incorrectly" fold. But so what? It is simply getting extra equity with everything else being equal. Unless you flop aces or better, your bet on the flop will always be one that you want him not to call (except for some of the rare times he has a deuce).

And what about those times you do flop aces? Check it, of course. He will probably bet it for you even with hands that he would have folded had you bet.

29. The following question applies to any stage of the tournament. You have been betting all the way against one player, who you think is on a draw. On the river you check, and he bets. Should you tend to call him with hands that cannot beat his draw if he makes it?

Answer: Although your opponents in tournaments will typically be more cautious than usual, this situation, in my experience, is an exception. I believe players in tournaments will bluff in this spot at least as often as they would in a sidegame. Of course, every player has to be evaluated individually. However, if this is a player you would call in this spot in a sidegame, I would definitely call him here.

30. As in the previous question, this situation can occur at any level of the tournament. Again you are betting all the way. But this time you think that your reasonably good hand is also worth betting on the river. When you bet, he raises. His raise represents a hand better than yours. So you can only beat a bluff. Should you tend to call?

> **Answer:** In the answer to the previous question I stated that in my experience tournament players are just as likely to make a bluffing bet on the end as they would in a sidegame. However, I believe a bluffing *raise* is a different story. Players who are trying to conserve chips are not anxious to throw away two precious big bets. So unless you have good reason to think otherwise about this player, I would tend to believe his raise even more in a tournament than I would in a sidegame. And, in spite of the pot odds, I would probably fold.

31. The game is seven-card stud. The stakes have reached $150-$300, with a $25 ante and a $50 bring-in. Your table is eight handed. You are down to your last $75, $25 of which you have antied. The player on your right brings it in with the 2♣. Your hand is the

Behind you are no tens or deuces, but there is an ace and a queen. Should you play?

> **Answer:** It is almost equivalent to the hold 'em situation in which there are two more hands before it gets to your blind.

If you don't play now, you will certainly have to play one of the next two hands. (The only difference is that if you play now, and win, you will win slightly more than if you wait until the bitter end, because your antes are dissipating.)

We learned in the text that, with one hand to go before your last hand, you should elect to play hands that are somewhat better than the average hand you would get if you waited until the end. With two hands to go you should play hands that are even better still, though not as good as what you would need under normal circumstances.

I do not believe that your pair of deuces is good enough to meet this criterion. I am almost positive that you are better off waiting, even though a pair only comes along about one in six times. The problem is that this pair is so small. So I think you should fold. However, it is close. And I would change my answer if any of the following five things were different:

1. Your pair was slightly higher.
2. There was no other deuce showing.
3. Your kicker was higher than any of the other upcards.
4. Some players had already folded. Or,
5. There was only one hand, rather than two hands to go before you were forced all in.

Again, if any one of these five things were true, I believe that would be enough to make you play.

32. In the middle of an Omaha high-low-split eight-or-better tournament, you have an average number of chips. You have the button. Your hand is

Before the flop the under the gun player raised and got five calls, including you. The blinds have folded. The flop is

The under the gun player bets, the next player raises, and everyone calls. So what should you do?

> **Answer:** This is not a case where tournament considerations can over ride your best play. Your hand is just too good. Furthermore, playing cautiously will not allow you to escape this hand before the river as it might in some other spots. You should reraise here. Period.

33. It is the middle of a limit hold 'em tournament. No one is on a short stack. Three people limp in, and you call in the small blind with

The flop is

Should you come out betting?

Answer: Almost definitely. Semi-bluffs on the flop in limit hold 'em would tend to work even better in a tournament than in a side game. By that I mean that one of the two aspects of a semi-bluff, namely the chance of winning immediately, usually increases in a tournament. The fact that an ace is on board also probably helps your chances of stealing the pot, since other players fear that ace if they don't have one themselves.

With a gut shot straight draw and a back door flush draw you will make a pat hand about one-fourth of the time you are played with. If you don't bet, you often would have to call if someone else did (or fold the hand you wish you could play). So it is usually better to bet yourself and give yourself the chance to win it right there. Another reason to bet is that hands like jack-ten will fold, which increases your chances of winning if you get called by something like a pair of eights.

34. Again, it is limit hold 'em. An early position player raises and gets three calls. The small blind folds. You call from the big blind with

The flop comes

Should you bet?

> **Answer:** Again, yes. There is a much smaller chance you will win the pot immediately, but it doesn't matter. It is still probably worth doing. The key here, though, is that an ace fell. By betting into everyone you will often make the raiser fold as good as a pair of kings. If you can do that, you might well win the pot instantly. Plus, a call from the other players can come with hands that you can beat if you catch as little as a ten or a nine. And as before, your bet will fold hands like king-ten or jack-nine.
>
> The only real risk in betting is that you will be raised, and then go on and lose the pot. EV-wise that possibly costs you a fraction of a small bet. Therefore, if your bet increases your chances of winning the whole pot just slightly, that should more than make up that fraction of a bet.

35. It is limit hold 'em, and again you have the T♦9♦ in the big blind against the same raiser and callers as the previous quiz hand. The flop is

Should you bet?

> **Answer:** Again, the answer is yes. In tournaments, the raiser on your left will often fold a pocket pair between nines and aces. Once you get by him you may win immediately. Even when you don't, you probably have five outs, plus a back door flush draw. Some of the times you don't win immediately, you are merely called by a hand that would have bet had you checked. So the bet cost you no more than a check and call would have. The fact that you might be raised is not a good enough reason, in most cases, to opt for a check with your hand.
>
> One important thing to realize about this hand and the two above it is that my admonition to avoid close gambles does not apply to those times that a gamble can increase your chances of winning the pot. Semi-bluffs early on should be made at least as often in tournaments as in side games.

36. It is a no-limit hold 'em tournament. There are 14 players left. The serious prize money starts being awarded to the nine players at the last table. The blinds are $100 and $200. The total amount of chips is $140,000. You have $15,000 in front of you. Both the small and the big blind have $3,000 in front of

them. No one is in and you are on the button, and hold

What should you do?

    Answer: Raise to about $900. I pick this number for a good reason. It needs to be high enough so that the two short stacks in the blind will be very reluctant to play unless they have a hand that is worth moving in before the flop. This is a very important concept. Had you raised a lesser amount, say to $600, they might call with hands like

or

with the intention of folding if they did not like the flop. Once you raise to $900 or $1,000, however, you have cut their implied odds and made them risk more money than they want to, (especially under the tournament circumstances), as far as flat calling is concerned. Thus, your raise has pretty much forced them to either fold or move all in.

A typical player in this spot will, in my experience, throw away about 90 percent of his hands. That means you will get away with your bluff about 80 percent of the time. Risking $900 to win the $300 blinds ought to be profitable.

Notice, however, that a somewhat bigger opening bet on your part is wrong. If you open for $1,200, you would practically guarantee that you would either steal the blinds or get moved in on. But those hands that would move in on you figure to remain the same, whether you bet $900 or $1,200. So the extra $300 that you risked, got you nothing in return.

I hope I don't have to spell out the fact that if you are reraised, you fold . Notice, by the way, that the fact you had J♠8♥was almost inconsequential. You will rarely see any flops, so you could have just as easily made this play with seven-deuce. And given the expected proclivities of the two players in the blind who are trying hard to make the last table, you should in fact play seven-deuce that way as well.

37. It is a no-limit hold 'em tournament with several tables left. When all the cards are out there is $1,800 in the pot. There are three hearts on board, but no pair, and your opponent checks to you. You have the nut flush. He has $1,200 in front of him, and you have more. How much should you bet?

Answer: The answer obviously depends to some degree on how the hand was played and who your opponent is. But I am trying to illustrate a specific concept with this question. Remember that one of the keys to good tournament play is to take advantage of the fact that your opponents don't want to go broke. (We assume there are no rebuys available.) That fact allows us to steal pots we might not ordinarily steal. In fact, in this situation, it might be right to move in if you had only the ace of the suit in question, but no flush.

However, you do have the flush, so the syndrome is reversed. We have to assume that this guy is less likely than normal to call an all in bet. $1,200 is not normally an out of line size bet given the size of the pot, but I don't believe it is the right bet in this spot. You need to give him hope to come back in case he loses. You should probably make a bet that will leave him with some chips — somewhere between $500 and $800.

38. It is the middle of a limit hold 'em tournament. No one is on a short stack. A player raises under the gun. All fold to you. You have

in the big blind. Should you call?

Answer: Absolutely not. This is a simple example where the right play is clearly different in a tournament than in a side game. 90 percent of tournament players need a better hand than usual to raise under the gun. Furthermore, they will play those hands cautiously. That means that if they have a pocket pair and an ace flops, you will win less than you would in a side game. Meanwhile your chances of flopping a ten and having it be a loser is greater than normal, as is your chance of flopping an ace and having it be a loser. Add all of that to the fact that you are trying to avoid close gambles, and you have a clear cut fold. In fact, I almost asked this question with you having ace-jack, rather than ace-ten. That would be closer, but still would almost certainly be a hand to fold.

39. It is the middle of a no-limit hold 'em tournament. The blinds are $100 and $200. Four people fold to a player who makes it $800 to go, and has $10,000 left. You know that he is aware of the Gap Concept. No one calls until it gets to you. You have

on the button and $4,000 in your stack. What should you do?

Answer: I believe this is one of those times you should move all in. Had his raise been larger, there would be no question about it.

We know he is raising with a lot of hands. So we cannot fold. If he had opened for, say, $1,500, it would be quite wrong to flat call. The flop might be a tough one to play, so you would rather be all in, or better yet, have him fold immediately.

However, when he raises to only $800, many players would be inclined to merely call and see what comes. That might very well allow them to conserve $3,200 in chips. I don't agree.

Again, I want to reemphasize that my admonition against close gambles that might make you broke does not apply to times that a close gamble can win you the pot without a fight. If you move in here, he will fold a large percentage of his hands. Those times he doesn't fold, you will win somewhat less than half the time. But all told, you should still show a nice profit.

Had you had, say, $7,000 in front of you, rather than $4,000, the right play would have more likely been to simply call. Moving in $7,000 is a lot more risk for essentially the same reward. And raising only $4,000 is really the same as raising $7,000, since if he did play, he would undoubtedly move you the rest of the way in. But when you have $4,000, your raise is exactly within the range that I recommend in the text, somewhere between two to fives times the size of the pot.

40. You are down to three players. The leader has $25,000 in chips, you have $15,000 and the other player has $5,000. The prize money is $10,000 for first, $5,000 for second, and $3,000 for third. The other two players are good friends and would rather not play against each other. They point out that you are exactly in the middle between first and third, and ought to finish second, so that $5,000 is what they offer you to end the tournament. Your buddy, meanwhile, points out that if all three of the players had $15,000, they each would average a third of the total or $6,000. Since you do in fact have a third of the money, he says $6,000 would be the fair settlement. Who is right?

Answer: You ought to win this tournament one out of three times. When you don't win, you will probably be against the short stack (for second place) that you now have a 3-to-1 chip lead over. A good estimate of your possible results would be that in 12 such similar situations you would win four, and of the remaining eight, come in second, six times. Thus, four times you would make $10,000, six times you would make $5,000 and two times you would make $3,000. That adds up to $76,000 over 12 tournaments, or an average of $6,333.

$$\$6,333 = \frac{(4)(\$10,000) + (6)(\$5,000) + (2)(\$3,000)}{12}$$

That is quite a bit more than the $5,000 they offered you. It is not surprising.

What might be surprising, however, is that even your buddy's recommendation was too small. The reason has to do with the fact that you have a better chance of playing for the top prize than you would if you all started out equally. To make this clear, suppose the leader had $29,000, while the other guy had $1,000 and you still had $15,000. You still have a one-third chance of winning, but your chances of coming in third have gone down further still.

Again, I want to say that the mathematical method that was used in this problem is not perfectly accurate, but it is close enough.

41. It is somewhere toward the end of a seven-card stud tournament. No one at your table is on a short stack. A 2♦ brings it in. A couple of small cards fold; and a player with a Q♠ showing, raises. This player is very familiar with the Gap Concept. Behind him is your 7♥, followed by the J♠ and a 9♣. You have

should you call, reraise or fold?

Answer: This is unquestionably a reraising situation. There is a very good chance that the queen has a worse hand than you. And if it is in fact two queens you are facing, you have a king kicker, which makes you only a small underdog if the hand is played heads up. Also, a key point is that your reraise will almost certainly result in a heads up pot, even if there is a pair of jacks or nines behind you. No way will typical players call with those hands, especially in a tournament, since they not only fear your reraise, but also fear the player who made the original raise with the queen.

If instead there had been an ace showing behind you, your reraise would have been much more debatable. Not only because the ace could have aces, but also because the queen would less likely be semi-bluffing with a weak hand.

42. It is the last table of a no-limit hold 'em tournament. The blinds are $500 and $1,000, and there is a $200 ante. The average stack is $30,000. You have $10,000, which is the shortest stack. The next shortest is $13,000. You are dealt

under the gun. What should you do?

Answer: This is a close decision between all three alternatives. Actually there are four alternatives because if you choose to raise you might raise either a small or large amount. In fact, if you had lots of money in front of you, you might well make it $3,000 or $4,000 to go. The problem with that play when you only have $10,000 total, is that you cannot fold if you are reraised.

Therefore, if you do opt to raise, you might as well move in right from the beginning. That play has the advantage of getting some hands that you want out. For instance, a pair of nines or king-queen suited is apt to fold to the bigger raise, but not the smaller one.

What about just calling? That is a definite alternative when there are few players raising before the flop, especially when you have a lot of chips in front of you. The idea would be to call, hope no one else raises, and enjoy high implied odds. With only $10,000 in front of you, however, you cannot get great implied odds.

It still might be worth a mere call if you're putting a lot of emphasis on moving up the prize ladder, but again, only if there are few players who are preflop raising. Given you are at the last table at this tournament, that is not likely to be the case.

Since it is likely that a limp on your part will be raised, might that indicate that it is better to simply throw the hand away? That would depend on the chip and the prize situation. If there is a reasonable chance that players will be going broke before you have anted off your money, you may very well want to fold here. Then again, it would probably be better, even in this situation, to limp for $1,000, hope you won't be raised, but fold if you are.

But in this specific case you have the lowest stack and can expect the slightly bigger stacks to wait you out. With that $3,000 or so sitting in the pot, I believe the best play is to just move in. You could easily win it right there. And even when you are called you will sometimes have the best hand.

I would change my answer to limping and then folding to a raise if there was no ante or if the other short stacks were gambling it up. But in the typical scenario I'd push in my $10,000.

43. It is the middle of a limit hold 'em tournament. A player in middle position raises, and you are the only caller, with

in the big blind. The flop is

How should you play the flop and fourth street?

> **Answer:** Check raise on the flop, and then bet all the way. This is often the right way to play in a side game as well, but it is definitely the right way in a tournament. The two alternatives of betting on the flop or waiting to check raise on fourth street are both quite wrong.
>
> Betting out on the flop can be right in a side game against an aggressive player who smells weakness and will raise with almost anything. That doesn't happen nearly as much in a tournament. Thus, you should check, knowing that with that flop the raiser will almost always bet.
>
> Waiting until fourth street to check raise gains a small bet over my suggested play when it works. The problem is that your opponent will often check the turn after you have called him on the flop, especially in a tournament. If instead your flop check raise ties him into the pot, you have gained three or even five small bets by playing the hand this way.

44. You draw a very tough table in a seven-card stud tournament. It will be many hours before it is broken up. A 2♣ brings it in, a Q♦ raises, and four others call. You have

and no nines or sevens are showing. One spade is out. What should you do?

> **Answer:** Reraise. Normally I recommend that you stay away from close gambles. And this certainly is one. Not only are you risking more money on third street, but your raise increases the pot to a size that may well force you to gamble heavier later on. But that doesn't matter. You have a slight edge and you should push it in this spot.
>
> Remember that the reason not to push small edges early in a tournament is because you are the best player, so it is worth giving up that edge to conserve chips against your opponents. But in this case you have little or no edge against your opponents. The players at the other tables might be a lot weaker, but you are apt to be gone before you have a chance to play against them. Had this question said that your table would be breaking up soon, I would have recommended a flat call on third street, giving up a bit of EV to ensure a decent stack size when you moved elsewhere. But with the question as stated, you can't do that.

45. Omaha high-low-split eight-or-better. You are on the button with

Three people limp in. What do you do?

Answer: Notice that I did not give any of the specifics of the situation — how many chips you or your opponents have, how they play, or how far along the tournament is. That is because it does not matter. You raise. End of story. (I have sprinkled a few questions like this throughout the quiz because I want to emphasize that strategy changes for tournaments almost always involve close plays only. This play is not close, and it would be hard to imagine a situation where you wouldn't raise.)

46. You are in the big blind with

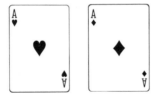

in a no-limit hold 'em tournament. A middle position player raises your $100 blind to $400. Everyone folds. You and he both started with $5,000 in front of you. What should you do?

Answer: One thing you should not do in a tournament is flat call. That play would be okay in some side games, where the object of course is to trap him later on. But that is not a good idea in a tournament. First, he is less likely to bluff off significant money. Second, he is less likely to call a decent size bet or check raise from you later on without having you beaten. Third, this trapping play entails small risks of losing a lot of chips — something to avoid in a tournament.

So we see the right play is almost definitely to reraise. The question is, how much? The answer depends on what hands he will call various size raises with. But before we examine that, something must be pointed out. Namely, that it is disastrous to give away our hand with a small reraise. This statement is less true when we have position, but in this case it cannot be emphasized enough. The reason it is so disastrous is that he can beat us out of so many chips. Therefore, reraising say, $500, while making it obvious we have a very big pair, can't be right. It gives him too good implied odds. Knowing what we have, he will most likely lose no more when he loses, but cripple or bust us when he wins.

Might merely moving in be the right play? It sure might. Suppose, for instance, we know he will call such a move in with a pair of kings. On the other hand, if we raise $1,500, he will call with either kings or queens. Depending on post flop play, it might very well be better to move in and hope you catch him with those two kings.

The problem with moving in is that most players will fold even two kings in that spot. And it would be a shame to waste aces by just grabbing the few hundred dollars already in the pot. It would be nice to make more when he does have a decent hand. Except we don't want to give him good enough implied odds to make his call right.

If we assume that after our preflop reraise we always move in on the flop, it is a simple matter to calculate what that preflop reraise needs to be to ensure that no hand is getting good enough implied odds. Basically we are talking about him having smaller pairs. From his perspective, if you will always move in the rest of your money on the flop, his implied odds are $5,400 compared to your reraise. Do you see why?

If he calls your reraise and wins, he will beat you out of your $5,000, plus the $400 he already put in the pot. If he loses, he loses the size of your raise. That's why reraising $500 is not enough. His implied odds are $5,400-to-$500, or almost 11-to-1, which would make calling with any pair correct. If you reraise $800, he is making a slight mistake. So slight, that given your tournament goals, you might rather he fold.

Once your reraise gets to about $1,000 you surely want him to call, knowing you'll move in on the flop. Therefore, the answer to this question is to reraise at least $1,000. But even that might not be enough if you think he is almost as likely to call a bigger reraise.

47. You are playing a satellite and are down to the last two players. The blinds are $50 on the button, and $100 in front of the button. You both have $1,000 left, and he moves in on the button. You know he makes this play with any pair, but nothing else. Do you call $900 more with

Answer: Obviously no one can be figured out this perfectly. So this is really more of a math question involving the ace-king. We are also not going to adjust for the fact that you might be the better player. You don't have enough money for that skill difference to mean much, unless he is throwing way too many hands away preflop. The only question here is whether ace-king will win often enough against a pair to justify taking the 11-to-9 odds you are getting.

First, notice that 11-to-9 means you must win 9 out of 20 to break even. That is 45 percent. I don't want you to try to do this question absolutely perfectly. You can't bring a computer with you to the table anyway. You should come very close, however, knowing just a few facts. They are:

1. Ace-king suited is about even against two deuces.
2. Ace-king suited is about 45 percent against two queens.
3. Ace-king suited is about 34 percent against two kings.
4. Ace-king suited is about 12 percent against two aces. And,
5. Two aces and two kings come up half as often as usual — three combinations versus six — when facing an ace-king.

Let us now estimate our chances. When the opponent has a pair below kings, your chances range from 50 to 45 percent. It is only slightly inaccurate to say that your average chances against these 66 combinations of pairs are 47.5 percent. Against the two big pairs your chances are an average of 23 percent. Altogether you will win 23 percent of the six combinations of big pairs; (that is 1.38), and 47.5 percent of the 66 combinations of smaller pairs, or 31.35. Altogether you would win 32.73 out of 72 combinations. Since 45 percent of 72 is 32.4, it looks like we barely have a call.

$$32.73 = (66)(.475) + (6)(.23)$$

$$(32.4) = (.45)(72)$$

The main reason I bothered you with this problem is to show you that you cannot get too worried about running into aces or kings when you have ace-king. In this example you are 47.5 percent when you know you are up against a pair below kings. Not knowing drops your chances down only very slightly.

48. It is the last table of a no-limit hold 'em tournament. There are five players left. The three players behind you have about $20,000 each. The player on your right has $70,000. You have $60,000. The blinds are $1,000 and $2,000. The chip leader makes it $12,000 to go under the gun. You have

What should you do?

Answer: Throw those two jacks away. You are not getting good enough implied odds to try to hit your set. And to try to win this hand without improving is too risky.

There are three players who will probably go broke soon. You have a good chance of coming in second, maybe first, and almost certainly, at least third. Your playing two jacks without improvement could easily result in slipping all the way to fifth. This question is a classic example of avoiding someone who can bust you in no-limit, especially when most of the other players cannot.

49. It is the middle of a limit hold 'em tournament, and no one has a short stack. A tight player raises under the gun. The next player reraises. You are next with

What should you do?

> **Answer:** If this is a major tournament with good players, you have an easy fold. You are getting no where near your odds to make a set. And if you don't make a set, you're in trouble. Especially if your opponents are capable of trapping. By that I mean they check aces or kings to you when the flop comes rags. If you were all in, you would have a close decision. With money in front of you, it isn't close.

50. It's the middle of a limit hold 'em tournament. Someone raises before the flop; someone calls, and you call on the button with

The flop comes

The first player bets, the next player folds. Should you raise?

Answer: Yes. This is a routine play that is often done in the hopes of getting a free card if fourth street is a blank. The down side is that good players will often reraise which makes your strategy backfire, unless you make your hand. However, in tournaments, where most players are playing cautiously, getting reraised, even by an overpair, happens less frequently. At least that has been my experience. Thus, I would tend to make this play more in a tournament than in a side game.

Hand Quizzes
Afterthought

I suspect that many of your answers will be different from mine. This is particularly likely if you are a successful sidegame player with only limited (or perhaps no) tournament experience.

These "Hand Quizzes" clearly illustrate the tremendous difference between tournament poker and what you face in a normal game. You are still playing poker, but it is a different form.

So if you had some trouble with the questions, read through them again and pay special attention to where the appropriate tournament concepts come into play and where standard sidegame strategy "goes out the window." Don't get discouraged if many of your answers are different from mine. In time, they will be the same.

Part Five

Questions and Answers
by Mason Malmuth

Questions and Answers

Introduction

David has covered a great deal of material in this book. However, for many people, reading and learning can be two different things. Consequently, to help you retain some of the more significant ideas, I have reiterated them in a question-and-answer format.

I suggest that, after you have read and studied the text, you try to answer the following questions. You probably will want to go over them many times. In addition, I suggest that you cover the answer that immediately follows each question. Only look at the solution after you have answered the question to the best of your ability.

Also, I want to point out that what follows is not a substitute for the text. In fact, some of the ideas in the text are not contained here. But enough material is included so that after you have thoroughly digested the text, the questions should help keep your tournament poker sharp.

Finally, the questions and answers are organized by topics covered in the text, so you can easily return to the appropriate section for a fuller explanation.

EV

1. What does expected value mean?

   The amount you will average winning or losing, per bet, if you could somehow make it a large number of times.

2. Why is it not always right to choose the play with the highest EV?

   Because the higher EV bet may be more likely to lose.

3. What if you have enough money to withstand short-term fluctuations?

   In that case it is always better to choose the bet with the higher EV.

4. What if you do not have that cushion?

   It may well be right to choose the slightly smaller EV if that bet will win more often.

5. When is this especially true?

   If going broke keeps you from making lots more positive EV bets.

6. What is a major factor involving EV in proper tournament strategy?

   Balancing your quest for extra EV and your quest for survival.

You're Broke
— You're Done

1. How does the way tournaments are typically paid influence your strategy?

   You should avoid close gambles with a slight advantage.

2. When does this take on most significance?

   Near the end of a tournament.

3. What is another reason to eschew close gambles even early on?

   If you are one of the best players in the tournament.

4. When can it be mathematically correct to pass up a mathematically good bet?

   If losing that bet can keep you from making an even better bet later on.

5. What if you have a heads-up situation with a hand that is only barely worth playing, EV wise?

   You seriously consider folding if losing that pot would get you broke or nearly broke.

6. What if you have a decision to slowplay a good hand?

   Assuming you are one of the best players in the tournament, many prospective slowplays should not be made.

7. When does this principle apply?

   Only on close decisions.

8. When do you gain a lot from deception?

Anytime you can deceive your opponents at lower stakes to the point where they will make a mistake against you once the stakes are raised.

9. What if your risk is small?

The idea of avoiding close gambles doesn't apply.

10. Example?

Seeing the flop with 3♥3♦ getting debatable odds.

11. What can you expect if you have the smallest stack at the last table?

Most of your opponents will be playing conservatively, hoping you go broke.

12. What should you do?

You must take chances and hope to get lucky.

13. What if other small stacks are foolishly playing too loosely?

The above strategy totally reverses.

14. Do the concepts in the chapter apply when you are thinking of betting or opening?

Not always. You will not play *fewer* hands (when first in) than you would in a normal game, but in fact, most likely play *more*. The avoidance of close gambles applies only to calling or betting in spots where you know you will be called.

They're Broke
— They're Done

1. What is quite common to see in a tournament?
   A player who is notorious for his looseness in normal games
   playing significantly tighter when he has a small or moderate
   stack.

2. What do you need to notice about your opponents?
   How tightly they are playing and play accordingly.

3. What do the most successful tournament players do?
   They aggressively go after small pots and quickly back off at
   the first sign of strength from their opponents.

The Gap Concept

1. What important first round principle is understood by all good poker players?

    You need a better hand to play against someone who has already opened the betting than you would need to open yourself.

2. What is the "Gap?"

    The difference between the hand you need to call (or raise) an opener with and that with which you would open yourself.

3. What does the width of the gap depend on?

    How tight your opponents play.

4. What if your opponents are quite loose?

    There may be no gap at all.

5. What about in a tournament?

    The gap is often extremely high.

6. What should you do differently than usual?

    In a tournament, it is often right to open raise with hands far inferior to those which you would need to call.

7. Hold 'em examples?

    If three people fold, you should probably raise with Q♣J♦ or 5♠5♥.

8. What if the under the gun player has raised, you are next, and you hold A♦K♥?

    Consider folding it.

9. When playing stud, what if you have the highest card showing (not duplicated elsewhere) and no one, except the bring-in, has entered the pot?

You should usually raise.

10. What if someone else raises in front of you?

You should usually fold any pair lower than the denomination of the upcard that had raised.

11. What about drawing hands?

Be less apt to play hands such as J♥8♥5♥ or three straights.

12. What if the players behind you have either a very small or very large stack?

Loosening up on your normal opening requirements may be unwise because you are less likely to steal from them.

13. What are exceptions to the Gap Concept (where someone else has opened)?

If the raiser in front of you has a lot of chips, or if he is not worried about going broke, *or* if he is aware of the Gap Concept.

Prize Structure Implications

1. What are you rooting for at the last table?
   For someone else to go broke.

2. What is bad to do late in a tournament?
   To risk large sums on near break even situations.

3. But what if you have a half decent edge?
   It could still be wrong to gamble.

4. What if you are the one who makes the first bet?
   By being the "aggressor," you find yourself more likely than usual to win small pots.

5. What is the bottom line here?
   The Gap Concept becomes even stronger when players are in the money or close to it.

6. What should you do when against players who are aware of the disadvantage of fighting close decisions when others gain by watching?
   You can aggressively steal small pots, even if they suspect that this is what you are doing.

7. What if it is the other player who raises?
   You need an even better hand than usual to play.

When They Call You

1. What two facts have a significant impact on your later round play, especially the second round?

    You are raising with *more* starting hands than you might normally be used to, and that they are calling your raises with *fewer* hands.

2. What if your hand is quite good?

    Be prepared to sandbag more than usual.

3. Stud example?

    You raise with <u>7♣K♦K♥</u> and are called by <u>? ?</u> Q♠. Since he is more likely than usual to have queens, you should try for a check raise on fourth or fifth street.

4. Hold 'em example?

    You raise with A♦A♣. The Flop is Q♣3♠2♥. You bet (the flop) and get called. You should go for a check raise on fourth street.

5. What if your hand is merely good?

    You should often immediately go into a check calling mode.

6. Hold 'em example?

    You raise with A♦J♦, get called, and the flop is A♣T♠4♥. Proper tournament strategy is to frequently go into a defensive shell and just check and call.

7. What if your hand is worse than usual?

    Be prepared to "be done with it" on the next round.

8. Why is firing at least "one more barrel" usually not right in a tournament with a weak hand?

 You must take into consideration the necessity of conserving chips, the fact that you are up against a better hand than usual, and the fact that your hand is not as good as it normally would be.

9. What is an important exception to the above regarding hold 'em and Omaha high-low-split eight-or-better?

 When ragged small cards come in hold 'em, or ragged big cards in Omaha high-low-split eight-or-better. In that case, you can bet a weak hand twice.

10. Hold 'em example?

 You raise with Q♣J♥ and get called. It is probably worth taking a shot at the pot when the flop is 8♣6♠4♥.

Chips Change Value

1. How does the value of each individual chip that you win compare to the previous ones?

They are worth less.

2. What is the bottom line?

With few exceptions, what you gain by winning a chip is not quite as much as what you lose when you lose a chip.

Keeping the Pot Small

1. What does an extra raise on your part do?
   It changes the nature of the whole hand from that point forward.

2. What does a bigger pot do?
   It causes everyone to stay in longer.

3. How does that affect you?
   You might have to take cards off that you would not have had to, had the pot been smaller.

4. What are the implications of bigger pots?
   Your opponents will chase more often when you have the best hand and might win a pot that you would have won.

5. What's another reason to keep the pots small?
   Opponents' hands are easier to read.

The First Level

1. In the larger tournaments are your results at the first level important?
   No. They are almost inconsequential to your eventual chances of winning.

2. What does this mean?
   You may want to consider playing a much looser style than you will in succeeding levels.

3. What is the reason for this?
   You are trying to create an impression that you can take advantage of when the stakes rise.

4. What do you do at the succeeding levels?
   During the second and third level you revert to tighter play, while from the fourth level on you would typically continue to play tight, but make more frequent aggressive stabs at stealable pots.

Limping

1. In a limit hold 'em tournament how often should you limp when no one else is in?

Rarely.

2. Why?

There is simply too great a chance that you will steal the blinds if you raise. Meanwhile, multiway pots are much rarer in tournaments which gives you less reason to limp with hands that prefer them.

3. Examples?

Hands like Q♠J♠ or 7♣7♦ under the gun, if played at all, should usually be brought in with a raise.

4. What about when playing seven-card stud?

You still limp fairly often.

5. Why?

Since one of your cards is showing, you cannot as easily represent a powerful hand when your upcard is small.

6. Example?

You have a live three flush, with a small card showing, such as J♥8♥4♥.

7. What if your three flush was with a high upcard?

We revert back to the Gap Concept and will raise more than we would in a sidegame.

8. In hold 'em what if someone limps in in front of you?

You must tighten up as opposed to being first in.

9. Be specific?

If your hand is merely good, you should be more apt to simply limp behind them rather than raise.

10. Example?

If a good player limps in first position usually fold K♥Q♦ (but call if the hand was suited) and call with A♣Q♥.

11. Stud example?

If a small card limps, don't raise without a big pair.

12. What about no-limit hold 'em?

It is different. The best players should be doing a lot of limping even with mediocre hands.

13. Why?

The Gap Concept doesn't apply in the early rounds of no-limit where the stack size is great compared to the blinds.

When Will
Your Table Break Up?

1. If your table will break up soon, what obvious effect on your strategy does it have?

You make no "advertising" plays.

2. What if your table is scheduled to break up soon, and you are playing against much tougher opponents than the average player in the rest of the room?

Stay away from close gambles.

3. What if you find yourself at a tough table that will not break up for quite awhile?

You can't play extra tightly in the hopes of conserving your chips for a different table.

4. What if you will have to play at a table for a long time?

Setting up plays for the future is even more important than in regular sidegames because the play you set up will most likely be at bigger stakes.

Adjusting Strategy
Because the Stakes Rise

1. What if it is near the end of a tournament, you have a small stack, and the stakes will soon rise?
    You should avoid taking risks in marginal situations at the lower limit.

2. Why?
    There is a better chance you will be able to sneak into a higher money position at the higher stakes when the stacks that are slightly ahead of you are apt to bust out.

3. What is the biggest reason to change your strategy as a result of subsequent increases in stakes?
    The payoffs from creating an impression early are greater than they would be in a normal ring game.

4. What if you play somewhat aggressively, or even wildly, early on?
    This results in getting calls down the road that you otherwise might not have gotten.

5. Why does this strategy pay off more in tournaments than it does in a normal game?
    Because those calls will be at bigger stakes.

6. What is an alternate strategy?
    To play very tightly, and even timidly early on, in order to set up a bluff down the road.

7. Which of these two alternate strategies should you use?

As a general rule, you should use the first strategy in no-limit or pot-limit tournaments, and the second strategy in limit tournaments.

Noticing the Short Stacks

1. What typically happens to players with much less than the average amount of chips in front of them?

They are ready to give up.

2. What does this mean?

It is often unwise to make your usual semi-bluff thrust at a small pot.

3. What is another reason to notice whether you might be up against a short stack?

So that you can adjust your hand selection towards starting hands that do well "hot and cold."

4. To what game does this concept mainly apply?

Hold 'em, especially no-limit hold 'em.

5. Example?

J♠T♠ is normally much better than A♣9♦, but not if you are running the cards out against the kind of hands (such as king-ten or king-nine) that a desperate short stack might call you with.

6. Should you make sub-optimal plays simply because they might help eliminate a short stack?

Almost never.

Noticing the Large Stacks

1. Are players with large stacks afraid of going broke?
   Most are not.

2. What are the implications?
   They are likely to call you with mediocre holdings or initiate the betting with such holdings.

3. How, in general, does it affect your play?
   You need to loosen up slightly when they open the pot, and tighten up slightly when they are behind you and you are considering opening.

When the
Blinds are Coming Up

1. There is one hand to go before your blind, and you have only enough chips to put in that blind when it comes to you. What should you do?

Play hands worse than you would normally play, but not merely better than average.

2. With one hand to go before your blind at a full hold 'em table should you play Q♠8♥ or Q♠5♠ if the blind will put you all-in?

No.

3. What would you need?

Something along the lines of king-nine offsuit, queen-ten offsuit, or jack-eight suited.

4. What if there is more than one hand to go before you are forced to put in the blind or your final ante?

The degree you loosen up would be even less.

5. What if you can wait four or five hands?

There should be almost no change in your strategy compared to normal.

All-In Strategy

1. What is one of the major differences between regular poker games and tournament poker?
   In tournaments, a player is often all-in.

2. Should you start playing poor hands when your stack is short?
   No.

3. If you are in the big blind, and all you have left is enough to call a raise, and a player is raising preflop either in the dark, or is in a strategic situation where he will raise with just about anything, what should you do playing limit hold 'em?
   Call no matter what you have.

4. When is the decision more ticklish?
   You have more than enough to call or it is a no-limit hand where his raise gives you less than 3-to-1 odds to call. Or, the hand you are facing is to varying degrees better than random.

5. What if you are playing no-limit?
   The size of your opponent's raise now becomes very relevant.

6. What does that mean?
   Even if you think he will raise with anything, you should still throw away your worst hands when his raise will put you all-in and give you odds of 2-to-1 or worse.

7. Suppose you have some inkling about what type of hands your opponent will raise you with?
   You can, in theory, calculate which hands to call with based on his possible holdings and the odds you are getting.

8. In hold 'em, what are the effects of future betting?

Certain hands go down or up in value.

9. Examples?

A hand like 7♠6♠ is rarely worth playing all-in, whereas A♥9♣ or K♥T♣ may well be worth moving in with, even though they should usually be folded if more chips are at risk later.

10. In seven-card stud, if an all-in pot seems imminent, how does it affect hand values?

Small and medium pairs go up in value, while small three flushes and three straights go down.

11. Examples?

You might play a hand like <u>5♥9♦5♠</u> but throw away a hand like <u>5♥9♥3♥</u>.

12. Omaha high-low-split eight-or-better example?

A♣K♠J♥4♦ is probably worth playing all-in, even in spots where it would normally be folded.

Just Out of The Money

1. If you are one of the short stacks, should you alter your play to try to sneak into the money?

If you are only concerned with maximizing your EV, you should.

2. What if you choose to make no adjustments?

You will much more often come in one out of the money, but occasionally reach one of the higher prizes.

3. What can you do if you are concerned about getting into the money?

Check the other tables and notice how your stack compares to everyone else's.

4. What if your stack is bigger than the stacks of one or two players at the other tables?

Assuming we are talking about stacks that are so small that losing one hand will deplete it completely, you should stay away from all close gambles and maybe even some not so close.

A Special Last
Two Table Situation

1. What will the short stacks do when the combination of the two tables is imminent?

They will tend to throw away all but their very best hands.

2. What should the chip leader at the table do?

Raise with an awful lot of hands.

3. What about the player with the second largest stack?

He is in a similar position, provided that the largest stack has already folded.

4. Suppose the shortest stack raises almost all-in. What should the chip leader do if he holds a hand like Q♥Q♣?

He should probably fold.

5. Why?

The gain from playing this hand is not worth having the tables combined and no longer being able to run over the game.

The Last Table

1. What is mandatory to take into account if you make the last table?

    The amount of money involved in moving up a place or two can be significantly more than the face value of the chips.

2. To whom do the strategy adjustments designed to move you up in standings apply?

    The players with fairly short stacks.

3. What if you have a moderate stack?

    You should make few adjustments.

4. Example?

    If there are nine players left, you have an average amount of chips, are in about fifth place, you could almost certainly ante your way into sixth prize. But given the increase in prizes paid to the last three places that are typical in most tournaments, any strategy along those lines would be ridiculous.

5. What is the major exception?

    When playing no-limit, and you are facing a stack that can bust you.

6. What is the basic idea when you are in next to last place?

    If you are in next to last place, but still quite short, you should tend to go out of your way to avoid going broke before the shorter stack does.

7. What if you have the smallest stack?

    The situation is the opposite. You should usually gamble, or at least not play any tighter than normal.

8. Why?

    Because it is likely that the player who has the second smallest stack is waiting for you to go broke.

9. What if the player with a slightly larger stack is disregarding you and still taking chances?

    Play extra tightly, and hope to sneak ahead of him.

10. Example?

    In limit hold 'em, fold Q♣J♥ if you're one to the right of the button with the second smallest stack.

11. But what if the smallest stack doubles up?

    The Q♣J♥ becomes a raising hand first in, especially if your recent play was very tight.

Down to Two Players

1. What's important?

   That you don't relax.

2. Why might you want to make a deal?

   By the time it is heads-up, losing two or three pots in a row that go all the way to the river will certainly eliminate the shorter stack.

3. If you don't make a deal, should you change your strategy from typical heads-up games?

   It depends on your skill level compared to your opponent's.

4. What if he is better than you?

   You must be aggressive.

5. What if you're the better player?

   Play your normal game, except you should try to avoid playing big pots with close decisions.

6. What is the only major mistake you could make heads-up?

   To play so tightly that you are destined to be ground down from ante steals.

Rebuy Tournaments

1. In tournaments where most people tend to rebuy if they go broke, what should your strategy be during the rebuy period?

    It should somewhat revert back to what you would use in normal games.

2. How do most players in a rebuy tournament play before their rebuy option expires?

    Significantly looser.

3. How does this affect your strategy?

    It shrinks the "Gap" in your opening versus calling requirements.

4. Should you rebuy if you are one of the better players in the tournament?

    Yes.

5. Should you add-on?

    It depends on how well you are doing.

6. What is a decent rule of thumb regarding proportional add-ons?

    To add-on if you have less than the average number of chips at that point, and not otherwise.

7. What if the tournament allows add-ons far in excess of the original buy-in?

    If you can afford it, and are one of the best players, you must seriously consider making this add-on, even if you are already doing well.

8. What if the tournament charges less per chip for your add-on than they do for your original buy-in?

You must almost always opt to purchase these cheaper chips.

Satellites

1. What is the proper strategy for a one table satellite?
   Somewhere between the proper strategy for a regular tournament and a sidegame.

2. When there is only one winner, how should you play in theory?
   Exactly as if you were playing in a normal game.

3. But what about in practice?
   You still have to worry about the fact that you cannot buy more chips.

4. What does this mean?
   You should avoid gambling in very close situations if you are a better player than most of your opponents.

5. Can you take advantage of the fact that your opponents are afraid of going broke?
   Many players don't worry about it. So you have to identify those who do. Then you will know who to apply the Gap Concept against and which ones not to.

6. What about super satellites?
   They are almost exactly the same as normal tournaments.

7. What if there are several winners, all of whom get the same prize?
   This forces you to sometimes play even tighter than in a normal tournament.

Making Deals

1. How much does playing superiority count for regarding deals?
Very little due to the size of the stakes.

2. What is the exception?
If your opponent folds too much.

3. When calculating the fair price of a deal, why can you not be precise when there are three players?
There is no ironclad way to calculate the chances of coming in second and third based on your chip position.

4. What happens in most three-way settlements?
The third guy tends to shortchange himself.

5. What's the best time to take advantage of this misunderstanding?
When you are the chip leader, or close to it, in a three-or four-way finish, especially if the shorter stacks are small, but not tiny.

Some No-Limit Observations

1. What tournaments are most profitable for the best players?
No-limit hold 'em tournaments.

2. When does the Gap Concept apply to these no-limit tournaments?
To larger opening bets or later rounds.

3. What if the opening bet is small?
If you are one of the better players, you can play a lot of hands that are cheap to come in with because of the edges you can obtain from future bets.

4. What about marginal confrontations against good players with larger stacks?
It is more important to avoid these confrontations in no-limit than it is in limit.

5. What about playing against small stacks who are trying to survive?
They are easier to take advantage of since they know you can bust them in one hand.

6. What about your knowledge of all-in prices?
It is rewarded much more in no-limit than in a limit game, since all-in situations and decisions as to whether to call all-in, or raise someone else all-in, come up much more often.

7. When does it hurt the most when someone makes a big bet or raise into us?
When we have a close decision as far as calling or not is concerned.

8. What if we know that we probably have a better hand than they do when they make that bet or raise.

We welcome the action.

9. What if their bet or raise indicates that we have no chance of having the best hand or drawing out?

That bet or raise does not hurt, since we fold.

10. How does it affect things when someone forces us to call when we are probably beaten or forces us to fold when we still had a chance?

It's very bad, especially in no-limit where a person can bet or raise an amount that puts maximum pressure on us.

11. What dose this mean?

With such hands we should usually avoid raising, check raising, or betting in last position since that will open up the possibility of getting reraised.

12. What is a common mistake made by beginning no-limit players?

To put in fairly big bets or raises before the flop with hands that are very good, but not so good as to welcome a reraise.

13. Examples?

Hands like T♦T♥ or A♥Q♥.

14. What are the three reasons that ace-king prefers to be all-in before the flop in a no-limit game?

1. It will sometimes be the best hand, even without improving, when all the cards are out.
2. Most of the time that ace-king wins it is with one pair — a hand that is very tricky to play.
3. A large percentage of the time that ace-king wins a showdown it will be when it caught an ace or a king on

fourth or fifth street. If it is not all-in, it will often not be around to catch those cards.

15. What is important to understand about ace-king?
    It is a lot better to be the bettor when you put all your money in rather than calling someone else's all-in bet.

16. What about ace-queen?
    It is quite a bit worse off than ace-king if one of the opponent's possible calling hands is ace-king. It is also twice as likely to run into a pair of kings.

17. When is the best time to move in with ace-king?
    When moving in is betting two to five times the size of the pot.

18. What if the bet is smaller than this?
    You will usually get called, especially when someone else has already bet.

19. What about raising or betting more than five times the size of the pot?
    That is also debatable because you might be risking too much to win too little.

20. So what should you do if you have significantly more than five times the pot and hold ace-king?
    You may decide that it is better to just call or perhaps raise a small enough amount that you can fold if reraised.

21. How can you negate most of a better player's edge?
    By getting all-in before the flop.

Questions and Answers
Afterthought

Again, these questions are not designed to replace the material in the text. Their purpose is to help keep you sharp between complete readings of *Tournament Poker for Advanced Players*. I recommend that when you believe you have become a proficient tournament poker player that you read the text material every other month and review the questions about once a week. Also, remember to cover the answers and to think through those questions that you have trouble with. In addition, attempt to relate the questions to recent tournament hands that you have played, and try to determine which concepts were the correct ones to apply.

Conclusion

As we have seen, at times tournaments are very different from normal poker games. It's no wonder that some people who excel at them do poorly in the standard ring games and vice versa.

It all starts with the prize structure and how the chips change value. Of course, the Gap Concept comes into constant play. And whether you have a short or a large stack, or whether your opponent has a short or a large stack, can dramatically impact your decisions.

But tournaments can really become interesting when there are just a few people left. Much can change on the turn of a card and some of our World Champions won their titles when they got lucky and drew out on that final hand.

But always keep in mind that tournament poker is, despite its differences, a form of poker. This means that you must be very skilled to achieve a high level of success. Those players who attempt to "fire away" almost always discover that they run out of chips, and those players who just try to survive, almost always discover that they didn't have enough chips.

Remember, when you're broke, you're done, and the same is true for your opponents. This fact dramatically changes play from a normal poker game and frequently creates a large Gap that you must exploit. Also, keep in mind that unnecessary, close gambles, even when you have the best of it, can be terrific mistakes in tournament poker, while the exact same plays produce much of your long term profit in the sidegames. Also, keep in mind that many of the tournament concepts we have talked about are relatively unimportant early in an event, but can make all the difference once there are only a few people left.

Yes, tournament poker can be a lot of fun, and these events can occasionally produce a big score if you are fortunate enough to win a large one. But they also require much skill, and being a successful tournament player requires much more than luck even though the luck factor can be very large in the short run.

In closing, I hope you found this book to be everything you expected, and I'll see you at the final table.

Index